CHANGE
HAPPENS

*Leading Yourself and
Others through Change*

MACK & RIA STORY

DEDICATION

To those with the courage to become comfortable being uncomfortable. A better life awaits you.

CONTENTS

INTRODUCTION

Although change is a constant in life, most people resist change. They resist what change brings, especially big changes. They fight to maintain the "status quo," even when it's impossible. We look at every change and immediately see how it will affect us. Unless we instantly see the change is positive, and sometimes even then, we fight to keep things the same.

Why?

Because change isn't comfortable. And, we all like to be comfortable. We work very hard to be comfortable in life. We go to school, so we can get a "good job" to buy a nice house, a nice car, and take a nice vacation. Many people spend years working in a job they don't like, so they can retire and be comfortable. Sometimes, we are willing to trade true happiness for security because it keeps us comfortable.

Regardless of how much we like or dislike change, it's certainly going to happen. We can't stop the clock or hit the pause button on life – it goes on. With that certainty comes the fact we must all deal with change.

What determines our ultimate success in life is how well we learn to adapt to the changes forced upon us, how well we learn to leverage change, and our courage to change. It requires courage to embrace change. It requires us to become comfortable being uncomfortable. It requires us to realize growth, personally or professionally, won't happen accidentally. If we aren't intentional, growth won't happen at all.

Mack and Ria have experienced a lot of change over the years. They both experienced personal transformation and overcame overwhelming odds to get to where they are today. Mack started out as a front-line, blue-collar factory worker who barely graduated high school. To escape years of sexual abuse, Ria left home at 19 with nothing.

Today, they live the life of their dreams, teaching and speaking on leadership, writing books like this one to help others, and traveling the world – together. They work with organizations to unleash leadership potential by taking complex leadership principles and making them simple to understand and apply.

They have lived through a tremendous amount of change in every area of life to get to where they are today.

Some changes weren't ones they chose, but they learned to adapt. Some changes, they learned to leverage. Some changes, they learned to create. Along the way, they realized applying the principles related to change helped them create the life they wanted, rather than the life they were given.

Mack and Ria want to share these principles with you because an "Abundant Life" is not just for some people – it's for anyone with the integrity, strength, desire, and the *courage* to claim it.

Living an Abundant Life, at work or at home with your family, is something they will address in this book. They will guide you through 15 principles of change and the key concepts that will allow you to lead yourself, and others, through change. They will share one principle in each chapter with two different perspectives. Ria's perspective focuses primarily on self and is followed by Mack's perspective which focuses on self and others.

The principles in this book are powerful – *when applied.* As with any tool in your tool box, it's only helpful when you use it. Like most principles, they are much easier to say than to apply. It can be done. However, the question is: Will you put them into practice?

Is it easy? No. Is it possible? Yes. It is possible to do more, be more, and have more in life. However, you must be unwilling to settle for being "comfortable." It's a choice. Choices always come with consequences. Choosing wisely brings the consequences we want in life. Choosing poorly brings the consequences we don't want in life. We certainly can't control everything that happens, but we can control the choices we make or don't make. Eleanor Roosevelt said, *"I am who I am today because of the choices I made yesterday."*

Who you are tomorrow is determined by the choices you make today. Choose wisely.

CHAPTER ONE
Nothing Fails Like Success:
Ria's Perspective

RIA'S THOUGHTS

"You can never get complacent because a loss is always around the corner. It's in any game that you're in - a business, game, or whatever - you can't get complacent."

~ Venus Williams

It's one of the greatest dangers success in life brings – complacency. Why? Because to become complacent means we quit striving for improvement, for growth, and for something better. Unfortunately, the risk of complacency rises with each level of success, personally and professionally.

We see it in sports teams, who come off a big win and simply don't put the same effort into winning the next game. We see it in companies that experience huge profits and expansions, then fail just a few years later, unable to sustain the growth. We see it in people who get promoted to a great job but fail to develop their skills enough to keep the job. Success is everywhere – and many times, it leads to failure because the individual, team, or organization becomes complacent.

Success often quickly leads to failure.

Complacency happens to organizations, companies, and teams because it happens to individuals. When we reach a goal, individually or collectively, we feel entitled to the rewards, including the right to rest on our laurels. The successful person "has arrived," and the temptation to enjoy what was earned, to rest, and to coast lurks just around the corner.

Past accomplishments should bring confidence, but all too often, they bring arrogance instead, causing pride. As you may know, "pride comes before a fall."

Successful people may forget what it means to be

hungry, and someone who isn't hungry won't fight as hard. Someone who isn't hungry won't be willing to sacrifice. Someone who isn't hungry won't give up in order to grow up.

Danny Miller talked about this in his book, The Icarus Paradox, where he discussed how corporate success often leads to corporate failure.

The problem with success and why it's often the precursor to downfall is because success often doesn't teach us anything. Success today is one of the biggest threats to future success because **we don't learn as much from it.** We can learn so much more from our mistakes, or our so-called "failures," and the lessons they teach us.

I bet if you have ever run out of gas, every time you got in the car to go somewhere for the next several months, or years, the first thing you did was check the gas gauge.

I remember the first time I got a bad sunburn. My grandmother took my brother and me on a trip to the lake. It doesn't take much to make two little kids happy – some water, sand, and a few beach pails kept us occupied for a long time. Grandmother wanted us to put on sunblock because we were there for several hours. I refused. At eight years old, I was sure I knew everything already.

I came back to the hotel that afternoon with blistered shoulders. I had been outside many times already that summer without being sunburned, but I hadn't been playing out in the lake and sun for hours on end until that trip. I spent the rest of the trip, and quite a few days afterward, wishing I had listened. But, I learned to listen the next time grandmother gave me advice.

We learn more from the lessons of failure because

they teach us principles. Success doesn't teach us what NOT to do, it teaches us what we did right at the time. That's a practice.

When we learn what worked once, we are learning exactly that – what worked once. It doesn't guarantee what worked once will work again, or in the future, or when some of the variables change. And, they will change.

What is required to become successful is not what is required to remain successful. In order to remain successful, there must be continued effort and improvement because change is going to happen, sooner or later, for better or worse.

The status quo in life is constant change. Children grow up, friends move away, jobs change, and people get divorced. As Benjamin Franklin famously said, "In this world, nothing can be certain, except death and taxes."

We know change is certain. Because change is coming, we know if we don't change too, success will certainly end in failure because nothing fails like success. Nothing fails like trying to stay exactly the same and not responding to the changes around you. Nothing fails like trying to remain the same in a changing world.

Complacency may be easy but it's fatal to long term success. Og Mandino said, "I will not allow yesterday's success to lull me into today's complacency, for this is the great foundation of failure."

You may have heard that a frog will not jump out of a pot of water when the temperature is raised gradually. If you dropped the frog into a pot of very hot water, the frog would immediately jump out by reflex. But when the water is cool to begin with when you place the frog in, and the change in temperature is gradual, the frog remains. And, dies.

CHAPTER ONE
Nothing Fails Like Success:
Mack's Perspective

MACK'S THOUGHTS

"Change is not required because survival is not mandatory."
~ Edward Deming

Everything around us is constantly changing and churning at an ever-increasing pace. Most of us struggle to keep up as the organizations where we work fight a constant, never ending battle to not be left behind by the competition or the next startup. But, at the same time, there are also some organizations and people that seem to always be ahead of the others. They don't appear to be struggling at all. They don't merely survive. They thrive.

How is it some organizations and people in the same industry thrive while those around them struggle to survive? It's simple to say, but it's not so simple to understand and act upon. Thriving organizations truly understand, better than most, *nothing fails like success.*

I remember the first time I heard those words spoken by Dr. Stephen R. Covey. He said, *"When a challenge in life is met by a response that is equal to it, you have success. But, when the challenge moves to a higher level, the old, once successful response no longer works - it fails; thus, nothing fails like success."*

When we can meet the challenge with an effective response, we are successful, but only for a brief moment in time because *everything* is about to change. In today's busy world, everything is constantly changing. People change, processes change, customers change, products change, demand changes, suppliers change, expectations change, and many other things will change.

When everything is constantly changing, the challenge is also changing. What was mastered successfully yesterday may no longer be relevant today. Therefore, the one thing that should also constantly change is *you* and *me.*

If we're not willing to change, we should expect to be left behind by those that are.

When we choose to constantly change to meet new challenges, we have a *chance* to continue to achieve personal and organizational success. But, when we refuse to change in response to new and greater challenges, we and the organizations where we work will struggle to survive, and some will end up taking a dive.

Once we've achieved success, most of us no longer want to change. We want to hold our ground and keep things just the way they are. After all, we've put in a lot of hard work and often suffered through many stressful days to be where we are. Once we become familiar with our job and the people we work with, we find our comfort zone. Most of us want to remain there.

However, at work, others are constantly making changes and asking you to make changes. Woodrow Wilson said it best, *"If you want to make enemies, try to change something."* Leaders in organizations make a lot of enemies because they have the responsibility of moving the organization forward. They are hired for that reason and are expected to help the organization and the team remain successful in the face of all of the change taking place inside and outside the organization.

I remember starting a new job at a new company. I was hired as an engineer and had to learn the system used to track costs, inventory, equipment, etc. There was a lot to learn. The bad part was the system was already obsolete and would be replaced with a new system within the next year.

After a month or so, I had learned what I needed to know about the new job and had mastered the system. I had it all figured out. I was once again on easy street. I could do my job effectively and efficiently. Success!

I was pleased. My new boss was pleased. He was glad he had hired me because I caught on quickly which made his job easier. In other words, I had been successful in my new role in the new organization for the new boss.

Then, everything changed for everyone. The old system was shut down and replaced with the new system. Instantly, everything was different. There was a lot of moaning and groaning throughout the organization.

I knew this would be my time to shine since I have always liked change and growth. While many others were complaining about the new system, I was focused on learning it. I knew if I could learn it quickly, I would be able to help others learn it, which would make me a more valuable team player. That's exactly what happened.

Before the change, everyone was successful. After the change, most struggled. What had gotten them there would no longer keep them there. Many people started blaming the organization and their boss for the changes. Blaming others when change happens doesn't increase your influence with the leaders. It decreases it. Your life will always be better with more influence, not less.

Alvin Toffler had this to say about change, "The illiterate of the 21st century will not be those who cannot read and write, but those who cannot learn, unlearn, and relearn." If you want to intentionally accelerate your climb up the corporate ladder and be recognized as a high impact team player by the high impact leaders in your organization, you must become a master at learning, unlearning, and relearning when change happens.

CHAPTER TWO
The Impact of Change:
Ria's Perspective

RIA'S THOUGHTS

"Change is the law of life. And those who look only to the past or present are certain to miss the future."

~ John F. Kennedy

The impact of change means the end of something familiar. When change occurs, the predictable, stable situation we have become comfortable with is ending and a new situation is beginning. For most people, that could be, *and usually is,* considered a negative impact of change.

However, there is also a positive side to the impact of change. Change brings new situations, new experiences, new challenges, and usually new opportunities. That could be, *although often isn't,* considered the positive impact of change.

The interesting thing is while we cannot control every aspect of the situation, we certainly can control how the change impacts us personally. To a large degree, how the change affects us is determined by our attitude and degree of acceptance of the change. Certainly, there will be changes in life you cannot control, and you don't see any positive outcomes whatsoever. At that time, you may choose to have a positive attitude or a negative one. And, the attitude you choose will determine much of what happens in the future.

Years ago, I started a new job at a hospital. I had been working there about six weeks when the director who hired me, and to whom I directly reported, announced her resignation. To say I was shocked, worried, and concerned about what would happen to me is an understatement. I had accepted the job expecting to work for and with her, and she was leaving!

It was a great decision for her. She had two beautiful

young children at the time, and she simply realized being at home with her children was more in alignment with her values.

I had the utmost respect for her decision – and still do – but I couldn't help but realize the change was going to impact me. Significantly.

Rather than hire another director to take her position, the senior leaders decided to have my department, and me, report to a director in another department. In addition to that, they allocated my hours to two different departments, so I now reported to TWO directors.

In just six weeks, I started a new job, in a new organization, started another new job, and reported to three different bosses.

My world changed drastically. Fearing the uncertainty of the future, I considered my options. They were limited. Resign and find another job, or stay there.

Another job wasn't a realistic option – I had worked and gone to school for years to get a position at that hospital. I wasn't going to let the impact of change take my opportunity away from me.

I realized the change brought about an incredible opportunity – if I chose to look at it like that. I could complain, be negative, and resentful about the changes in my world. Or, I could be positive, helpful, and embrace the changes.

I knew many people would complain under the circumstances. Some might even resign. I also knew *how* I accepted the changes would impact my future opportunities in the organization.

I chose to embrace the changes and to be positive about it. I learned all I could from both of my new bosses, eagerly taking on additional responsibilities. In just a year, I was promoted to manager of my department, and later director. Of course, if I had chosen to be negative about the changes, I would not have been viewed as someone with leadership potential in the organization.

Frequently, when change impacts us, we become more focused on the negatives of the situation instead of the positives. Often, we spend more time and energy worried about what we don't know and what we can't control than we do on looking for the benefits of the change. We will find what we are looking for. And often, what we are worried about doesn't come to pass anyway.

The impact of change can be enormous in life. I'm not disputing that in any way. I've gone through some major changes over the years and nearly every one of them brought some fear of the unknown.

Often, change brings some sadness with endings, but it can also bring joy with new beginnings. Sometimes, it's easier to see the opportunities, and sometimes it's not easy at all. Sometimes, we are tempted to hold on tight to what we know because it's comfortable and familiar.

Change always impacts us. The only question is: *how?* How we are affected is determined in large part by our attitude. Our attitude is determined by our thoughts about the situation. Choose to look for the bright side, and you will find it.

To those who choose to embrace change, the future is hopeful. For those who choose to be threatened by it, the future is fearful. To those who choose to look for the opportunities instead of the challenges in change, the future brings exactly what they are searching for.

CHAPTER TWO
The Impact of Change:
Mack's Perspective

MACK'S THOUGHTS

"The secret of change is to focus all your energy, not fighting the old, but on building the new."

~ Socrates

With over 11,000 hours of leading cross-functional, kaizen teams through change – process improvement and cultural transformation – I've seen it all when it comes to how people deal with change. Kaizen is a Japanese word that means continuous improvement or small change for the better.

For many years, at one point in my career, I would start each week in a new place with a new team implementing new changes. My job was leading people through change. The vast majority of them didn't want to change and didn't want to be a part of change. The impact of change brought out the worst in some and the best in others.

When change happens, the first thing people want to know is, "How is this change going to impact me?" Until they know the answer, they're not interested in anything else. It's the leader's *responsibility* to help others feel *safe* when change happens. If there's one thing you can count on, it's this: Change happens.

Jim Kouzes remarked, *"Uncertainty creates the necessary condition for leadership."* When people are uncertain about the changes happening to them and around them, there's a tremendous need for leadership. Leaders must help their team members focus on what's new and move beyond what's old.

When change happens, some people will simply go through the change passively allowing change to happen to them while others will grow through the change actively making change happen around them. Those growing through change will be identified by their leaders as high impact team players who are helping them and other team members effectively deal with change.

When change happens, those going through change tend to *whine*. But, those growing through change tend to *shine*. We want to help you shine because just as shiny objects get noticed, so do shiny people. When change happens, it's the perfect time to intentionally separate yourself from the crowd.

Change is a separator. Change will impact different people differently. We don't always get to decide what will change, but we do always get to decide how we will respond when things do change. In this book, we want to offer you a perspective on change that will allow you to leverage change for your benefit.

When you're able to see change as your friend instead of your enemy, you're able to make better choices.

You can choose to lead change, choose to avoid change, or choose to resist change. It's your choice. And, it's a choice that will have a major impact on your future career growth. High impact leaders in organizations notice those that lead change.

Typically, people respond to change in three ways. There are those that lead change. They are considered leaders, whether they have a leadership position/title or not, and make up about 15% of the group. Then, there are those who avoid change and will never change. They are the slackers, and make up about 15% of the group. What's left is the 70% in the middle. They will change, but they are *resistant* to change. They want to wait and see what happens.

Imagine for a moment, you're the leader of the organization, department, or team, and you're ultimately responsible for moving your team or group forward when change happens. Which team members can you depend on to help you? Those leading change? Those avoiding change? Those resisting change?

The answer is common sense, right? You depend on those leading the change. They will help you accomplish the mission. Those formally responsible for an organization, department, or team know one thing. If they don't accomplish the mission, their boss will find someone who will because moving forward is not an option. *To survive and thrive, change is necessary.*

When change comes to your area, how does it impact you? Which group do you typically fall into? Do you lead change? Avoid change? Or, resist change? Do you *whine*, or do you *shine*? How do you allow change to impact your career? Positively or negatively? It's your choice.

When it comes to your career, leaders are looking for those among their team who are willing to help them lead. Think about this. Will you be happier at work if you have more influence or less? More. Are you likely to be paid more if you have more influence or less? More. Are you likely to be promoted if you have more influence or less? More. More influence gives you more options.

In an organization that is constantly changing to remain competitive, who will have the most influence? Those leading change? Those avoiding change? Those resisting change? There's no doubt which group has the most influence. It's always those willing to step up and lead the way when change happens.

How will change impact you? I love Abraham Maslow's thoughts about change. He said, *"When we are faced with change, we either step forward into growth, or we step backward into safety."*

CHAPTER THREE
Two Ways to Deal with Change:
Ria's Perspective

RIA'S THOUGHTS

"You must take personal responsibility. You cannot change the circumstances, the seasons, or the wind, but you can change yourself. That is something you have charge of."

~ Jim Rohn

Viktor Frankl was a neurologist, psychiatrist, and a Holocaust survivor. He spent three years in concentration camps and lost most of his family, including his wife, there. He suffered intolerable abuse, starvation, freezing cold, and exhausting physical labor. He lost everything, including a manuscript he was working on.

With every reason to give up, he continued to have a positive outlook and find meaning in the suffering. One of his theories was man could withstand nearly anything if there was a *reason* for it and a *why* behind it.

After Frankl was released, he published several books, writing about his experiences and what he learned from them. In one of my favorite quotes, Frankl states, *"When we are no longer able to change a situation, we are challenged to change ourselves."*

He went on to explain, *"Between stimulus and response, there is a space. In that space is our power to choose our response. In our response lies our growth and our freedom."*

Regardless of the situation we find ourselves in, we have the ability to choose how we respond to it. Even if we cannot change the situation itself, we can choose to change how we look at it and how we respond to it.

When we choose to rise above our circumstances or our environment, we find the ultimate freedom in personal growth and development.

Stephen R. Covey wrote about this concept in his book, *The 7 Habits of Highly Effective People.* In the book,

Covey explained when we choose our response based on values, we are proactive. When we choose our response based on emotions or feelings, we are reactive.

Viktor Frankl certainly didn't *feel* like rising above his circumstances. He certainly could have blamed many people for his suffering. Instead, he responded to his situation based on his values – choosing to be proactive, grow his personal strength of character, and rise above his circumstances to be positive.

In one of the best examples I have seen of someone choosing to be proactive, he chose to share his thoughts about learning from one's hardships and overcoming them. He recorded his observations on tiny scraps of paper and hid them, so he could keep writing. Those scraps later became a book, *Man's Search For Meaning,* after his release.

The proactive person will rise above his or her situation, take personal responsibility, and choose to be proactive by developing their character. The reactive person will blame anything and anyone else for their circumstances and choose to do nothing.

Often, we don't *feel* like being proactive. When the server gets your order wrong at a restaurant and your steak is well done instead of medium rare, how will you respond? A response based on your feelings of frustration and disappointment would cause you to blame the server, blame the restaurant, get angry, and become demanding. A response based on your values (assuming you value people) would cause you to assure the server you understand mistakes happen and politely let the restaurant correct the mistake.

Easier said than done? You bet. But, we all have two choices when it comes to dealing with change. We can be proactive, respond based on our values, and choose personal growth; or, we can be reactive, respond based on emotions and feelings, and choose to abdicate our personal responsibility for growth.

Here are three reasons why we should always seek to be proactive when responding to change:

1) **Being proactive will help you manage your emotions.** Your happiness is not dependent on your circumstances. That doesn't mean you aren't striving to improve, but it does mean you can learn to be grateful for what you have.

2) **Being proactive will allow you to stand out among your peers as someone who is a leader or who has leadership potential.** Those around you will realize you have good character and take responsibility for yourself and your growth. You will shine because not everyone will embrace change.

3) **Being proactive will help equip you to meet the challenges of change and turn them into opportunities.** Changes are not something to be afraid of but rather something to be hopeful about because there is potential for something better.

CHAPTER THREE
Two Ways to Deal with Change:
Mack's Perspective

MACK'S THOUGHTS

"Being intentional about discovering the hidden ways in which we sabotage ourselves empowers us to expose and eliminate these invisible culprits."

~ Amir Ghannad

Are you a model? I believe we all are because someone is always watching us. The real question is, "What are you modeling?" When change happens, you can rest assured those responsible for implementing the change are watching you. They want to know several things. Are you with them or against them? Can they trust you? Will you help them? Or, will you hurt them?

When change happens, do others see you whining or shining?

The instant change begins to happen, you begin to increase or decrease your influence with those around you because change puts you in the spotlight. Your peers are watching and your leaders are watching. When the spotlight is on you, the pressure is also on you. How will you respond? Will you be seen hanging with the whiners or hanging with the shiners?

Will you be proactive or reactive? When we're proactive, we respond based on values which are aligned with natural laws and principles. When we're reactive, we respond based on our feelings and emotions. Proactive people shine, and reactive people whine. Proactive people get results. Reactive people get frustrated.

As I discuss change with you, I'm going to assume one of your values is to increase your positive influence with those on your team who are growing through change and those in your organization who are responsible for leading change. I'm also going to assume you want to separate yourself from the whiners by leading yourself through change proactively.

To understand how to proactively deal with change, it will help if you understand how reactive people deal with change.

When change happens, reactive people instantly begin to let their feelings be seen and heard. They are the first to complain. They will be the most outspoken. There's one thing I know, *the more we complain, the less we obtain.* Their goal is to start the anti-change movement and to begin rounding up all the other reactive people. They complain together while working, at break, at lunch, and after work. Their goal is to maintain the status quo.

In the business world, *there's nothing worse for your career than to attempt to impede the forward progress of the organization.* There's no such thing as standing still in today's fast paced, ever changing world. You are either moving forward or backward. Anyone resisting change is trying to put themselves, you, and the rest of the team out of a job.

Reactive people are selfish. They don't look at the big picture. They don't value moving the organization forward. If they did, they wouldn't be reactive. They would be proactive. Reactive people value comfort not growth.

According to William James, *"Human beings, by changing the inner attitudes of their minds, can change the outer aspects of their lives."* This is the essence of becoming a proactive person. Proactive people take responsibility for their lives.

We can intentionally change the way we think, and proactive people do just that. As you read this book, you will have the choice to read it with a proactive perspective and choose to apply the principles in order to become a high impact team player. Or, you can read it with a reactive perspective and figure out all the reasons not to do what we're suggesting on these pages. The choice is yours to make.

Proactive people choose to *become comfortable being uncomfortable.* They want to make a difference. They are intentionally moving themselves, their families, and their organizations forward. They are living with purpose on purpose for a purpose. They make things happen.

Proactive people are not attracted to reactive people. When it comes to character, we are attracted to people who are like us. Therefore, proactive people associate with other like-minded, positive, proactive people. Reactive people associate with other like-minded, negative, reactive people. Which group is climbing the corporate ladder? Which group is constantly holding themselves back?

When major change comes to an organization, two groups quickly form. One group with the 15% who want to lead change proactively will get busy making things happen. Another group with the 85% who will be avoiding and resisting change get busy complaining about what they think *might* happen. It becomes one of those "us against them" situations. This happens whenever there is change within any size group.

High impact leaders are also proactive and invest their time and energy on the 15% who are helping them move forward. Important relationships are formed between the proactive people with more influence. Unimportant relationships are also formed between the reactive people with less influence. However, their reactive behavior insures their influence will continue to decrease rather than increase.

H. Norman Wright made a great point, *"You may not even be in a bad situation, but if you think you are, you respond as if you were."* Too many people listen to the wrong people.

CHAPTER FOUR
Resisting Change:
Ria's Perspective

RIA'S THOUGHTS

"The first step toward change is awareness. The second step is acceptance."

~ Nathaniel Branden

Resistance to change varies from person to person and from situation to situation. Some people are more accepting of change, learn to adapt quickly, and enjoy change. Others don't want changes of any kind, in any way, and won't change anything at all if they can prevent it. What's interesting is we can recognize this in other people's lives, but when it comes to our own, sometimes we don't even realize we are being resistant to change. Often, we resist change because we fear the unknown.

You have probably heard the expression, "Better the devil you know than the devil you don't know." Some people choose to resist change and go with a known situation, even if it's not the best choice.

For example, consider a college student choosing which classes to take next semester. A required biology class is offered Monday mornings at 8:00am or Thursday evenings at 6:00pm. The student has worked with the Monday morning professor before and knows passing that class would be easy. The Thursday evening class fits the student's schedule much better, but the student thinks "better safe than sorry" and enrolls for the known professor's class on Monday mornings. To avoid an unknown professor, the student re-arranges his or her entire semester.

If we are resistant to change for the sake of keeping things the same, we make the mistake of missing out in life. We stay in jobs too long. We stay in relationships too long. We stay in places too long. We become stagnant.

Last year, Mack and I moved from the house we had been living in for 13 years. It was a good move and an exciting new chapter for us, but it was a little intimidating to be moving to a new home, in a new city, in a new state, without most of the comfortable routines I had set up over the years. Where to grocery shop, which roads to take to avoid traffic, where I ran, where to buy gas, what restaurants to eat at, where to bank at, it all changed.

I found myself fighting a sense of mild panic at the thought of just how much life was about to change. It would have been very easy to focus on all the negative things about moving instead of all the positive things.

Some people, myself included, are hardwired to appreciate more structure, stability, and security than others. However, I've learned not to resist change because with change comes opportunity.

Nearly everyone experiences some level of resistance to change in some dimension of life. Maybe, it's not moving to a new city that gets you uncomfortable. Maybe, it's changing careers or changing what brand of shoe you like to wear, but nearly all of us have experienced resistance at some point or another.

Sometimes, resistance is based on a valid reason – I don't like to change the brand of running shoes I buy simply because I had some not so great experiences with other brands. Now, I only buy the brand I like, and I don't experiment. But, it's certainly possible I'm missing out on an even better brand simply because I don't want to try something new and risk something worse than what I have now.

Here are three reasons some of us resist change:

1) **It's not comfortable.** Anytime we are changing, we must get outside our comfort zone. We leave

behind a comfortable, familiar setting and find ourselves dealing with a lot of unknowns. It's like buying a new sofa. The new one is cleaner, nicer, fresher, firmer, and softer. The old one is worn, lumpy, torn, and stained. But, it *fits you better* than the new one. Eventually, you get used to the new one and don't think about it anymore, but it takes a little time to adjust and get comfortable again.

2) **It's not easy.** Anytime we are changing, we must put more energy into the situation. Change jobs, and you must learn a new set of skills or maybe a new computer system. Change cities like Mack and I did, and you must spend much more time thinking about where you are going and what road to take to get there. Change requires more energy and effort than the status quo because your brain must unlearn and relearn.

3) **It requires risk.** Most of us have a natural aversion to risk. I'm talking about the average person here, not someone addicted to the endorphin rush that comes with some activities, like Nik Wallenda walking across a high wire. As a rule, we don't mind risking often if the risk is small or low, and we don't mind risking as much when we stand to gain big. But, we don't naturally like to take risks if the odds aren't good, or we stand to lose a lot. Change brings about some risk because we might not like the new situation as much as we like, or did like, the old one.

CHAPTER FOUR
Resisting Change:
Mack's Perspective

MACK'S THOUGHTS

"Unfortunately, too often people focus on the negatives and lose sight of the multitude of blessings that surround us and the limitless potential that exists for the future."

~ Sir John Templeton

Whenever and wherever there is change, you will find a large group of resistant people. Some of them will surprise you.

I remember one organization where I was leading process improvement teams and also conducting leadership training classes. I was told there was a lady, Pat (name changed), who *needed* to attend one of my week long leadership development classes. So, I made sure she was enrolled in the very next one.

Before the class, I made sure I was able to meet her. I discovered she was one of the nicest and sweetest ladies I had met in the manufacturing plants. I was a bit confused as to why she *needed* to be in the class.

Fast forward to Monday when she arrived for the week long leadership development class. One of the first things I did to kick off the training was invite the participants to share what they thought about all of the changes going on and how they felt about being in the class. It allowed me and the group to get a sense of how everyone was feeling at the start of the week.

When it was Pat's turn to speak, she just sat there with her arms crossed and a scowl on her face. I had met her in private before. But now, we were in front of nearly 30 people. She was a very different person among her peers.

I didn't know she was very resistant publicly to all the changes that had been taking place. The changes I was leading. I also didn't know she was very reactive and vocal about her feelings to anyone in her department who would listen. So, here she was. That sweet little lady I had met previously, but she didn't want to speak.

Finally, after a little prodding, she opened up. She said, "This is what I think. I think this company is BS. Your program is BS. And, you are BS." Now, she didn't use the abbreviation. She just let it fly. She wanted everyone to know she wasn't on board. I don't think there was anyone in the room who missed what she had to say. She provided a perfect example of reacting based on feelings. She hadn't even considered her values.

By Wednesday, she had turned the corner. She came in with humility and shared some personal things with the group while tears ran down her face. By that point, the group had bonded around many of the principles I'm sharing in this book and many that aren't discussed here. Then, came the graduation on Friday.

At graduation, everyone had a chance to speak about how the week had impacted them and what they took away from the class. Many former graduates and many formal leaders attended these graduations. I never knew in advance what each graduate would say, so I was anxious to hear what Pat would share.

When her turn came, she walked forward with her head down looking at the floor. Then, she slowly raised her head and said, "On Monday, I walked in and told Mack he was BS, his program was BS, and this company was BS. But, I found out this week I was BS." She didn't use the abbreviation this time either. After making her short but powerful speech, she returned to stand with the group as they all took turns hugging her.

Most often, people are resistant to change because they haven't been taught how to think about change. When change happens, it's the leader's responsibility to insure his/her team is prepared for change. Daniel Burrus described perfectly what had happened over the course of the week when he said, *"Managers change behavior. Leaders change the way you think without you realizing it."*

Pat came in on Monday thinking one way and left on Friday thinking another way. Because she spoke with humility after she had done so much bad-mouthing of me, the program, and the company prior to her training, she made others pause and consider their own beliefs. She also probably didn't realize her impact. She was choosing to make the transition to join the 15% who wanted to lead and embrace change.

She had come in Monday with influence among those who were choosing to avoid and resist change. That influence wasn't worth a lot relative to helping her advance her career. But, she didn't know what she didn't know. However, she left having influence among the leaders. She had positioned herself with a new group.

Switching groups isn't easy. It's hard, especially if you've been bad-mouthing those leading change. However, it's absolutely worth it if you want to take control and responsibility for advancing yourself and your career.

The story about Pat reminds me of something I read recently from John G. Miller. He wrote, *"God grant me the serenity to accept the people I cannot change, the courage to change the one I can, and the wisdom to know...it's me!"* That's a powerful thought. It's also a proactive thought.

Are you a part of the right group? If not, are you willing to go within and make the necessary changes? Those avoiding and resisting change are toxic to your career. If you can't help them, you must leave them behind.

CHAPTER FIVE
Change or Be Changed:
Ria's Perspective

RIA'S THOUGHTS

"In times of change, learners inherit the earth; while the learned find themselves beautifully equipped to deal with a world that no longer exists."

~ Eric Hoffer

Early in my career, I was working as a manager for a franchise. We had a small team of managers, just four of us. We all worked closely together to keep the organization running smoothly.

If one of us wanted more than one day off, we had to make sure none of the other managers were planning to be off. That way, there were always two managers scheduled to work and one in reserve.

The store manager was the top manager on site. I, along with the other two managers, reported to her. I always worked the day shift, opening the store every morning and preparing for the customers. I was always following the night manager Joe (name changed), and whatever shape the store was left in when he closed would be what I had to deal with the next day.

Joe loved to have a good time at work. He loved people and tried very hard to make everyone happy. Often, that meant giving away free stuff to customers and employees, even though it wasn't his to give away. Joe liked to be the good guy. Unfortunately, he liked making everyone happy more than he liked making sure the work was done.

I had only been working there a few months when I started to notice a pattern. When I opened the store after Joe had worked the night shift, things would be missing. The cash register wouldn't be balanced or closed out correctly. The store wouldn't be clean or stocked. The time sheets would be a mess, and no one had taken their breaks or clocked out early when business was slow.

I wasn't the only one noticing these things.

Our store manager asked Joe to come in early for a shift one afternoon. No one else would be working, and the store would be slow. I was asked to be a witness for HR documentation purposes. Firmly, and with kindness, she laid it all on the table for Joe to be sure he knew where the problems were.

Joe wasn't meeting expectations. He wasn't following the (very few) rules we had about giving away freebies to employees and customers. He was trying hard to be friends with the employees and was crossing the line from leader/manager to buddy. Discipline problems were showing up in the form of poor customer service.

In the past, Joe's lack of leadership and management skills had not been as big of an issue because the previous franchise owners had lower expectations.

But, we had a new franchise owner. The new owner had high expectations, higher requirements, and lower margins. They expected all of us to follow the standards. Joe needed to change in order to keep his job. If he didn't change, he would be changed.

Joe needed to unlearn his old style of management and leadership, learn a new set of skills, and install some discipline on his shift in order to overcome his too-friendly relationship with some employees.

He would also need to change his focus from having fun to getting results. He needed to change his habit of oversleeping sometimes and being late for a shift. He needed to change leaving the store messy for someone else to clean up on the next shift. Joe needed to change his character.

Joe was receptive to the feedback from our store

manager, and he really tried to improve over the next few weeks. But, he really didn't like to tell anyone "no," and the employees knew it.

Things weren't getting better; they were getting worse. Joe eventually decided he didn't want to change. When confronted with the decision, he refused to change and was forced to resign.

Joe had learned to get along ok with the previous ownership. But, Joe wasn't able to (or wasn't going to), unlearn, relearn, and change his behavior, style, and character to meet the demands of our new culture.

When things change, we can decide to change with them, or we will find ourselves put aside, passed over, or pushed out.

When we are put aside and passed over, we may never even realize there was an opportunity, and we missed it. We become quietly overlooked once we're identified as someone who refuses to change when necessary. Opportunities and promotions may go to someone with less experience or seniority simply because they demonstrate the ability and willingness to change.

When we are pushed out, we find ourselves fired, terminated, asked to resign, or asked to retire. Often, although not always, that's the result of continuously refusing to change over time.

In times of change, we must be able to meet the demands of a new reality. Or, we will become obsolete.

CHAPTER FIVE
Change or Be Changed:
Mack's Perspective

MACK'S THOUGHTS

"Most people won't pay the immediate price to change and end up paying the ultimate price for not changing."

~ John C. Maxwell

Don't let John's words slip by without slowing down and reflecting on them. The principle he reveals is powerful. When change happens, we are going to pay the price of change one way or the other. I'm sure you've heard the old saying, *"You will pay now, or you will pay later. But, you're going to pay."* This saying is based on the same principle.

The price, relative to change within your organization, refers to two main areas:

1) **Time/Energy** – This is a *fixed price* and must be paid whenever you decide to change.
2) **Influence** – This price is a *variable price*. Timing is huge in this area. If you lead change and/or accept and embrace change early, you may actually *receive* a payment with an increase in influence. However, if there's any delay in accepting, embracing, and supporting the change, you will *pay* a price by losing influence. You may never know you have lost influence, but it will happen. *The longer the delay, the greater the loss.*

I'll assume you're going to *change* at some point, instead of being *changed* at some point. When you *change*, you are accepting the change before being terminated. When you are *changed*, you have refused to change and are terminated/replaced. Leaders always prefer to *change* you (help you change) rather than have to change *you* (terminate/replace you).

When a person refuses to get on board with change, they are choosing to potentially self-terminate. Of course, they will blame the boss and the organization because that's what reactive people do. They blame others for their circumstances. They transfer responsibility.

However, when change happens, you'll notice the proactive people are not terminated/replaced. They continue forward in their career with the organization. It's the reactive people who always have issues.

As I mentioned, the longer you wait to accept, embrace, and support change, the *less* influence you will have. If you plan to stay with the organization, you're losing influence not only now, but also in the future. *Don't wait to change.* The sooner you accept, embrace, and support change, the *more* influence you will have.

And for those who simply refuse to change, they will most often pay the *ultimate price* and lose all of their influence because they will likely be terminated/replaced at some point. They may even lose influence outside of the organization.

How could that happen? Because if their next employer requires a referral from their last employer, they won't get one, or it won't be a good one. Or, the future employer may know someone at their previous employer and ask them for a referral behind the scenes without the applicant's knowledge.

Influence is hard to come by. I highly recommend maintaining what you already have and growing your influence when you can. Your choices will ultimately determine your influence at home with your family and at work with your team.

There's no reason to delay accepting, embracing, and

supporting change because doing so will only reduce your influence. Less influence leads to fewer options. Less influence leads to lower pay. Less influence leads to fewer promotions. Less influence leads to more frustration. Less influence leads to more stress.

Some may say, "I've resisted change and didn't lose any influence." To those I say, "Oh yes you did! You just didn't know it." It's a principle. When you resist change initiated by leaders, you lose influence with those leaders. Not some time. Every time. Whether you know it or whether you don't, it's going to happen.

I've had the privilege of working in front line, entry level positions as a machine operator in organizations, and I've coached, mentored, and trained executives and owners at the top, along with all those in between. I've made a career out of leading others through change and transformation at all levels.

This has given me behind the scenes insight that many don't have. I've heard the closed door conversations about people who resist change. I've also seen the opportunities they missed but never knew they missed. I've heard the discussions about who gets a raise or who doesn't and why. I've heard the discussions about who gets promoted or who doesn't and why. These people never had a clue how much their choices were costing them. They most likely will never know. They'll think, "That's just the way it is." Our choices determine our results.

What are your choices costing you? Do you really *know*? Or, do you *think* you know? When it comes to change, I think Les Brown nailed it when he said, *"You're either in the way or on the way."*

CHAPTER SIX
If You Snooze,
You Will Lose:
Ria's Perspective

RIA'S THOUGHTS

"Because things are the way they are, things will not stay the way they are."

~ Bertolt Brecht

I remember when my grandparents decided to sell their house and build another one. They wanted to move away from the city to a quieter place in the country. That meant selling the house they had been living in for over 20 years. In fact, they had been living there since I was just a year or two old, and all of my memories of them were in that house.

Isn't it strange how, when things change, we naturally think of how the change will affect us first. I was more worried about the nostalgia of losing the house where all my memories were made than I was about how great the move was going to be for them. In fact, I couldn't believe they didn't ask for my permission before moving!

Anytime change is occurring, there are challenges and opportunities. Those who are quick to grasp the opportunities will be able to take advantage of them, while those who are resistant to change will come late to the game.

I started teaching group fitness many years ago because I enjoy it, and it helps me stay in shape. At the time, the gym manager who hired me was also an instructor and my mentor as I started teaching. She played a huge role in helping me learn to be successful in teaching and set a great example for all of the instructors.

About six months after I started teaching, Jane (name changed) resigned. A new manager was hired almost immediately. But, this new manager had different ways of doing things. New policies, new schedules, new everything.

I didn't like it. I didn't want things to change. I wanted the new manager to handle everything just like Jane had. I wasn't happy about things changing, and I wanted everyone to know it. I thought maybe if I pouted enough, things would stay the same. Then, I wouldn't have to deal with the changes.

Looking back now, I'm not proud of my attitude at the time. I could have done so much more to embrace the change and make the new manager feel welcome. Instead, I let my frustrations about the change be known.

It took a long time for me to realize I was the one with the problem. It also was a long time before I realized I had missed a valuable opportunity to grow my influence and build a relationship with the new manager.

Instead of focusing on moving forward, I was dragging my heels and kicking to keep moving backward. I got exactly what I wanted – the new manager knew I didn't like change. That meant I was one of the last ones to know about any changes that occurred from then on. There wasn't any need to seek feedback from me or ask for my input on making things better at the gym because I was resisting change.

I did eventually learn my lesson and realize that regardless of my wishes, change was going to occur in life, at work, and at home. I also realized I was missing out by refusing to embrace changes when they occurred. I was only hurting myself with my attempt to maintain the past.

The longer it has been since there was change, the more difficult it will be to accept it when it does occur. Maybe, that's because we think we earn more of a right to maintain a situation as time goes on. We must realize we aren't entitled to the status quo.

It gets easier to accept change when it occurs more often. Once we have gone through a change, we realize it may be uncomfortable for a time, but we can become comfortable being uncomfortable. That allows us to adapt better in the future.

We have all heard the saying "The early bird gets the worm," usually from a well meaning older relative intending to encourage us to get up early. But, it's just as relevant when it comes to change.

The first person to respond positively to change has first dibs on opportunities that come up. Opportunities to stand out as a leader, opportunities to influence others around you, opportunities to have input or help make decisions, and opportunities you can't even see yet. In other words, *if you snooze, you will lose.*

We all are in favor of improvements when they benefit us, but sometimes we refuse to give change a chance if we can't immediately see the benefits. It's true. Change isn't always for the better. It's also true that if nothing changes, nothing gets better. If everything stays the same, there will be no improvement.

New technology is a good example. Consider those who refused to buy a car when they first came out. Then, consider how strange that seems today in light of how cars are an integral part of our transportation system.

If we are slow to respond to and accept change, we lose out on precious opportunities. Even if we can't see them yet, they are there and usually only available on a "first come, first served" basis.

CHAPTER SIX
If You Snooze,
You Will Lose:
Mack's Perspective

MACK'S THOUGHTS

"Difficulties come to you at the right time to help you grow and move forward by overcoming them. The only real misfortune, the only real tragedy, comes when we suffer without learning the lesson."

~ Emmet Fox

For some, change is a major difficulty. For others, they don't even notice there was a change. They quickly observe, adapt, and move forward like it never even happened. They don't lose a thing, but they gain a lot because they're out front leading the way.

These are the same people who have the most influence in what changes will and won't be made in the organization. However, those who choose to struggle and resist change, most often, find themselves on the outside looking in. They don't usually have any input in the changes taking place. They must simply deal with it. They are usually the thorn in the sides of those leading the change. Some even relish this role.

They are the worst. They not only do not want to change, they want to gather up as many supporters of the status quo as possible. They truly believe strength in numbers will help them prevent the change that is in front of them. These people aren't moving themselves and their organizations forward. They are asleep at the wheel.

I don't know about you, but if I'm going to ride with someone, I don't want them asleep at the wheel. Actually, I prefer to be driving.

What about the people who don't get it? What about those who refuse to get with the new program, refuse to adjust to the new way of doing things, or refuse to adjust to the new boss? What happens to them when change happens? What impact will they have? What price will they pay?

Change can fuel our growth and advancement in the company if we learn from all the lessons we'll receive once we accept, embrace, and support change.

You have nothing to prove and everything to lose by being hard-headed. Trust me. No high impact leader will ever be impressed by how resistant you are.

However, those who avoid and resist change will make you feel like a hero. You don't want to be a hero to those people. They can't help you because they won't help themselves. They like to stir up trouble and don't mind using others to do it. It's not about you. It's about them.

When it comes to change, you really will lose when you snooze. Here are seven ways you will lose when you choose to snooze:

7 Ways You Lose When You Snooze

1) **You will have less meaningful, positive influence in every direction.** Why would anyone want to choose to decrease their influence? When your influence goes down, so does your value and your options.

2) **You will not be asked for input.** One way a decrease in influence reveals itself is when your boss and other leaders don't ask your opinions or let you know what's going on. They don't want to talk with those who are focused on figuring out *why* new things *won't* work. They want to talk to game changers who will *make* new things work.

3) **You will be passed over for promotions.** Why would anyone responsible for leading and implementing change consider promoting

someone who is resistant to change? They wouldn't. When you resist change, it's like letting everyone pass by you in the amusement park lines and wondering why you never get to ride anything. It doesn't make a lot of sense.

4) **You will be passed over for pay increases.** Some people don't want the responsibility that comes with a promotion, but most people do want a pay increase. The impact of resistance to change is the same in this area as it is for promotions. The people who support and embrace change will be rewarded. Those that don't will get passed over.

5) **You will be seen as part of the problem instead of part of the solution.** The impact on your career is magnified behind closed doors in conversations you may never know about. When it comes to change, leaders are constantly discussing who is on board and who is not. Why? They want to know who is helping them and who is hurting them.

6) **You may be demoted.** This doesn't happen too much because if you choose to be a part of the problem, you're a part of the problem regardless of your position.

7) **You may be terminated.** The ultimate loss. Not only do you pay the price of your choices, but now those in your family must pay too.

It doesn't have to be this way. In the words of Jerry Sternin, *"It's easier to act your way into a new way of thinking, than think your way into a new way of acting."* Knowing is not enough. You must act on what you know.

CHAPTER SEVEN
The Challenge of Change:
Ria's Perspective

RIA'S THOUGHTS

"God grant me the serenity to accept the things I cannot change, the courage to change the things I can, and the wisdom to know the difference."

~ Reinhold Niebuhr

I read that approximately half of Americans make a New Year's Resolution in January. And, only about 8% of them actually achieve it.

Most resolutions are related to goals we all want to achieve – a better lifestyle, more time with family, a healthier body, more exercise, more sleep, etc. Resolutions worth keeping in other words. Yet, the vast majority of people will not be successful because resolutions require change. And, change is hard even when we want it. It's especially hard if we don't want it, or it wasn't our idea.

Last year, Mack and I moved to a new city. As I unpacked and set up in my new kitchen in our new home, I realized the silverware holder wouldn't fit in the drawer I wanted to put it in. So, I put the silverware on the other side of the kitchen, near the sink, where it would fit.

A couple of months passed before buying a new silverware holder made it to the top of my priority list. I finally found one that would fit in the drawer where I wanted the silverware. It didn't take long to transfer the silverware to the new drawer by the stove.

I finally had my kitchen set up exactly how I wanted it. The silverware was now in the most logical place and where I had planned for it to go all along.

More than six months later, I still find myself opening the wrong drawer at times. The silverware was only there for a couple of months, and it was out of the way over there. It doesn't make sense for it to be in that drawer. Yet, I still find myself going out of my way to open the wrong drawer, only to realize a hand towel will not help me eat my salad.

Change of any kind always brings with it the challenges of adapting to something new. It requires us to use more of our conscious mind than our subconscious mind. Habits that served us in the past are no longer helpful.

Habits are those routine actions and responses we perform over and over again to help us automate something. Habits free up our mind to focus on something else, so we aren't wasting the energy needed to save the world on thinking about tying our shoelaces.

The challenge of change comes in consciously thinking about our new reality. Whether it's changing our eating habits to lose ten pounds or changing our attitude towards our new boss, we must *consciously* change ourselves.

It's like walking into a room in your house. When it's daylight, you walk into the room and do not need to do anything in order to be able to see. The sunlight passing through the windows allows you to navigate quite well without turning on the light. However, if you walk into that room after it gets dark outside, you cannot see the furniture and must take action – turn on the light – in order to see.

When we want to change something or respond to a change in our environment, we must realize the old situation is similar to walking into the room when it's daylight. We didn't have to do anything to function. But, the new situation is like walking into the room when it's dark. We must take action in order to respond to the new reality. It requires extra effort and energy. It won't happen accidentally.

This is difficult when we desire the new reality. It's much more difficult when we tell ourselves we don't want the new reality.

How do we overcome the challenge of change? We start by maintaining a "big picture" perspective of what we truly want. We must have a bigger, burning desire inside to help us be successful in changing ourselves. The desire to change has to be based on an intrinsic (internal) inspiration instead of an extrinsic (external) motivation.

External motivators will keep you motivated for a short time, but they aren't enough to truly affect behavior, thoughts, or an attitude change. Intrinsic inspiration is the only driver for lasting change within.

For example, written goals are much more likely to be accomplished because writing something down helps you "buy in" to the possibility.

I've seen this over and over in the thousands of hours I've spent teaching and coaching.

Change is a challenge because it forces us to cross the gap between knowing and doing. It requires us to take action and change something within, so we can change something without. It's much easier to cross that gap when we know *why* we are doing it.

When we have a long-term perspective of the potential for improvement that comes with the change, we will be subconsciously much more bought-in to changing. That makes it much easier to bring our thoughts and actions into alignment and will help us be successful. It's not easy to do. When we truly value the end result, we will make it happen.

CHAPTER SEVEN
The Challenge of Change:
Mack's Perspective

MACK'S THOUGHTS

"Progress is always preceded by change. Change is always preceded by challenge. Where there is no challenge, there is no change. It's the job of the leader to challenge the process."

~ Andy Stanley

If you want to continue to get the same results you're getting today, then you do not have to do anything differently. You're safe. You will never have to change a thing. Right? Wrong.

I've often heard it said, *"If you always do what you've always done, you will always get what you've always gotten."* That would be absolutely true *if* everyone else continued to do what they've always done. That would mean we live in a world where nothing changes. But, we both know we live in a world where everything is changing. Not only is everything changing, but it's also changing rapidly.

Therefore, if you always do what you've always done, you will get *less* because those who are changing for the better will get *more* of everything. If you want a better career and more out of life, change is not an option. It's required.

If you want slightly different results, then you must do things slightly different. But, if you want dramatically different results, then you must do things dramatically different. The question you must ask yourself is this, "Do I want a little more out of life?" Or, "Do I want a lot more out of life?"

Regardless of where you are in life or when you ask yourself this question, the answer will always determine the amount of change required to get the results you want.

If you're earning $50,000 a year and want a little more

out of life, you must change a little. If you want a lot more out of life, you must change a lot. If you're earning $500,000 a year and want a little more out of life, you must change a little. If you want a lot more out of life, you must change a lot.

Your ability to lead yourself and others through change will determine whether you get a *little* more out of life or *a lot* more out of life. You must *challenge* your own process. The process of *how you think* about change. You must step outside of the frame, so you can see the whole picture. Ria and I are on a mission to help you see the whole picture, the big picture.

Today, you may hate change, resist change, or simply prefer not to change. But, if you want more out of life than you're getting today, it's time you start *loving* change. This means you're truly becoming comfortable being uncomfortable. You expect change. You support change. You willingly and energetically make changes. You even suggest and champion change.

When it comes to climbing the corporate ladder and the pay scale, those who *love to change* get a free pass to the front of the line. Think about it. If you were a leader responsible for leading and challenging the process, which type of people would be the most valuable on your team? Those who love to change, or those who hate change, resist change, or prefer not to change? It would be those who love change. Not some time. Every time.

The Founder of Chick-fil-A, S. Truett Cathy, got it right when he said, *"We hear of businesses succeeding or failing, but it is not the business ... it is the people who succeed or fail."* It's all about the people. Truett and his team grew Chick-fil-A from a single restaurant to thousands of stores with annual sales topping $6 billion. We've been privileged to have them as a client for nearly three years now.

What do we do with Chick-fil-A? We support them by leading them through growth, change, and the development of their people. They are great, but they want to be better. That's what makes them great. They have people who embrace, support, and seek change constantly. Not just change, but rather, change for the better.

Businesses are trying to increase profits every day. Businesses are trying to increase sales every day. Businesses are trying to improve their processes every day. Businesses are trying to cut costs every day. Businesses are trying to attract new customers every day.

The more aggressive they are, the quicker they will be at making changes. The more successful they are, the more they will challenge their processes. The best companies are the companies that are the best at changing.

As you challenge how you think, I hope you will begin to see how your attitude toward change can impact your life for the better. Once you begin to challenge how you *think* and *act*, you will begin to be challenged in another way. Those who don't embrace change may stop embracing you and start challenging you.

When you start to lead yourself at a higher level, you will begin to gain influence with the high impact leaders and the decision makers in your organization. However, you may lose influence with those who don't want change. This is where your toughest battle may be.

Whenever you begin to grow and change, you may need to leave some people behind. Not because you're better than them, but because you're going in a different direction. John Kenneth Galbraith believes, *"Leaders stretch to meet the challenge. Followers shrink away from the challenge."*

CHAPTER EIGHT
The Fear of Change:
Ria's Perspective

RIA'S THOUGHTS

"Everyone thinks of changing the world, but no one thinks of changing himself."

~ Leo Tolstoy

Fear is what happens when anxiety over something becomes overwhelming. It's a strong emotion that can occur when we believe there is a possibility of a threat or a danger. What's interesting is we often spend a lot of time and energy being afraid of something that may never happen. In fact, *the vast majority of our fears are completely unfounded.*

When we fear change, we are afraid we won't like what is happening. When we fear change, we are fearful we will end up worse off than we are now. When we fear change, we fear a loss of some kind.

Change can bring fear when we form our identity around, or place our security in, something outside of ourselves.

For example, if your identity and your sense of self is centered on your job, then any changes involving your job can cause fear because the job defines you. If you lose your job, you lose a piece of your identity.

If your security is founded on family and your sense of self is based on your role as a parent, then fear can come when your children move away to college. They are moving away, and now, you must redefine your self.

If you place your sense of self on your internal values however, then your security is based on your inner worth. Your internal values will be the foundation for which you base your identity. An external situation won't have an impact. Changes in your environment won't rock your world in the same way they might have otherwise.

It's important to distinguish between fear and a sense of loss. If you are principle centered as a person, then your kids moving away to college won't shatter your foundation. Yes, of course you will miss them, and you will feel a little sadness. But, you will also experience happiness for them and their new beginning.

When I resigned from my career at the hospital in 2014, I was leaving a place I had worked for several years. There was sadness at the ending. I knew I would miss the relationships I had formed while working there. There was a strong sense of community and family in the organization. I was blessed to be a part of it for years.

It wasn't "just a job," and I knew there would always be some aspects of working there I would miss.

However, during my last few weeks, I realized something: My career is what I *do*. It's not who I *am*. My job doesn't define me as a person. Yes, there was some sadness over leaving. There was also a lot of excitement at taking a new step and starting a new chapter. I realized leaving a job meant both beginnings and endings.

I was much less fearful taking that step and becoming self-employed because I realized my value as a person wasn't determined by the job I had. My security in earning a living is based on my internal values. My success in earning a living isn't determined by the job itself. I determine my potential based on my work ethic, ability to work, determination to succeed, willingness to learn, desire to improve myself, and unwillingness to quit.

Anytime we are fearful of change, it's time to take a step back and look inside to determine why we are afraid.

Here are three common fears related to change:

1) **Fear of the unknown.** As people, we generally

like to know what's coming. Most of us don't like big surprises in areas truly important to us. We worry about what might happen. We spend time thinking "What if?" and frequently our fears are never realized. To overcome fear of the unknown, focus on the facts of the situation, rather than telling yourself a story that may not be true.

2) **Fear of losing control.** Having control means we can get what we want. More control equals more options. Life is better when we have more options! We love the freedom to make decisions. We fear situations where we lose control because we have fewer choices. To overcome the fear of loss of control, we must focus on what we can control about our situation, instead of what we cannot control.

3) **Fear of loss.** Think of the four year old little boy who learns he is going to be a big brother. Initial excitement starts to fade when he realizes his relationship to one of the most important people in his world is changing. He starts to become afraid of losing mom. Will she have time for me? What if she loves the new baby more than she loves me? To overcome fear of loss, we must focus on the gains change will bring, instead of the loss.

CHAPTER EIGHT
The Fear of Change:
Mack's Perspective

MACK'S THOUGHTS

"May your choices reflect your hopes, not your fears."
~ Nelson Mandela

If you're going to choose to fear something, don't fear change. Fear mediocrity.

At this moment, you may or may not realize how much the fear of change may be holding you back. Ria and I are intentionally raising your level of awareness relative to your ability to effectively deal with change. No matter who you are or what you've achieved, there's something more you want from life.

That little voice in your head is nudging you forward. It constantly plants and waters the seeds of aspiration within you. What is it inside of you that holds you back? What inside of you prevents you from actually climbing to the next level? It's one thing. And for everyone, it is the same thing. It is fear. It is *fear of change.*

You have much more potential inside of you waiting to be released. However, you must remove the barrier of fear that is holding back your potential. Do you have courage? Do you have the courage to let *"your choices reflect your hopes, not your fears"* as Mandela suggested?

There's only *one* person on this earth who can remove the fear barrier and allow you to climb to the next level and beyond personally and professionally. That person is you. Do you have the courage to unleash your potential? We hope you do. We believe in you!

Dale Carnegie observed, *"Courage comes with the sun. You can conquer almost any fear if you will only make up your mind to do so. For remember, fear doesn't exist anywhere except in your mind."* If you can get up, you can show up. Courage is revealed by the choices you make. Choosing to be fearful or courageous will be based largely upon the stories you tell yourself. Want different results? Tell yourself different stories. Want dramatically different results? Tell yourself dramatically different stories.

The most important person you will ever talk to is yourself. Be careful what you say because you are always listening. Sure, there will be others who talk to you. However, what they say does not determine what you do. What determines what you do are the choices you make based upon the story you tell yourself about what others say.

When it comes to excelling in the workplace, you must learn to ignore the voices of fear surrounding you. Have you ever noticed when someone is afraid they seek the safety of others? They want others to be with them and near them to make them feel safe. They want you to join them to validate and confirm their fear. They want you to be afraid too, so they will feel justified in their fear.

Fear of change in the workplace creates the same desire in others. You will be surrounded by the voices of those who fear and resist change. Listen to them:

- That won't work here.
- We've already tried it, and it didn't work.
- It's working fine just the way it is.
- We just started running smooth from the last change. And now, they want us to change it again?
- Have you thought about what will happen if we try this, and it doesn't work?
- Who came up with that brilliant idea?
- It worked better the old way.
- I'll try it, but it's a waste of time.

What do you tell yourself when you hear these voices?

Do you agree with them? Do you become one of the voices? Are you one of the voices? Lead yourself beyond your fear.

When I heard my long time mentor, John C. Maxwell, say, *"Leadership is influence. Nothing more. Nothing less."* I realized everyone is a leader because everyone has influence. His words inspired me to write my first book, *Defining Influence.* It's a manual on how to increase your influence in all situations.

Marcus Buckingham put it this way, *"Leadership is not reserved for leaders."* In *Defining Influence,* I ask the readers to consider where their influence is on a scale of 1 to 10. We all have influence, so we are all on the scale. We don't get to say, "I don't want to be a leader." The question is not are you a leader, but rather "What kind of leader will you be?"

When Marcus said *leadership is not reserved for leaders*, he meant, it's not reserved for those with titles or formal positions of authority. Leadership is for everyone. This entire book is filled with leadership principles to help you lead yourself and others effectively through change.

I love what Andy Stanley had to say about fear, *"You're afraid. So what? Everybody's afraid. Fear is the common ground of humanity. The question you must wrestle to the ground is, 'Will I allow my fear to bind me to mediocrity?'"* When you choose to avoid change, you may be choosing to embrace mediocrity. I'm sure when you hope and dream, you don't hope and dream of mediocrity. There's more out there for you.

My friend, Donovan Weldon, spoke these powerful words, *"The only person between you and success is you. MOVE! The only person between you and failure is you. STAND FIRM!"*

Will you embrace change? Or, will you embrace mediocrity? The choice is yours to make.

CHAPTER NINE
Embracing Change:
Ria's Perspective

RIA'S THOUGHTS

"Change before you have to."

~ Jack Welch

Learning to welcome change is quite different than learning to tolerate change. I remember learning in grad school about bell curves in the general population, where 15% of the population is considered "early adopters," those who eagerly embrace a new idea, technology, or concept as soon as they hear of it.

At the time, I realized I was not an early adopter by nature. I much preferred to let the early adopters "work out the bugs." When it came to new technologies, I never downloaded the first release of my new iPhone update – I waited until the ".1" version came out when I was fairly certain some of the initial problems had been worked out. I was not interested in the new features until I was confident the basic features would work. Reserved and cautious was my preferred response.

Then, I realized I was missing out sometimes because I simply didn't want to change or try something new. I avoided shopping at the new grocery store down the road simply because I had to learn where everything was. (Don't judge - for someone who writes her grocery list based on the aisle order, that was a pretty uncomfortable change.)

But, I was missing out on shopping in a new, nice, clean store, with grocery carts that didn't wobble when I pushed them.

It may seem strange for someone who didn't like change to write a book on dealing with change. But, I've learned we can embrace change in big and small ways. Every time we do, it gets easier.

Today, I look for ways to embrace change because it's an opportunity to try something new, learn something new, or discover something new. Does it always work out? No. Sometimes, I order something new at a restaurant, and I don't like it. But, I enjoy the experience of getting outside my comfort zone.

Here are five ways you can embrace change:

1) **Stop and think.** Action is the enemy of thought. Sometimes, we are so busy *doing* that we stop *thinking*. In times of change, spend some time thinking. Sit down somewhere quiet. Think about what's going right in your life. Think about what's not going right in your life. Think about what needs to *change*. Think about what you need to do in order to create that change. Reflection is pure gold when it comes to finding peace with change.

2) **Let go of the old.** It's strange how nostalgia makes the past seem better than it was. It's certainly ok to have those fond memories, but remember to keep them in perspective. Don't spend too much time looking back. Living your life looking back all the time is like trying to drive a car while looking in the rearview mirror. Resolve to remember the past, but let it go. Move on to the future. It wasn't as good as it seems now. Even if it was, it's gone.

3) **Remove the clutter.** Every time I move, I am amazed by the "stuff" that accumulates. A move is a great time to re-evaluate the physical baggage you are carrying around in the form of old

keepsakes or memorabilia and get rid of some of it. But, you don't have to move in order to improve your environment. It's not just physical either – improve your emotional environment by getting rid of the things that aren't serving you. Piles of junk in your hall closet aren't helping you embrace the future. Neither are any toxic relationships in your life.

4) **Try something new.** Go eat at a new restaurant. Order something you have never had before. Visit a new city or state. Read a book by an author you have never read before – maybe you will gain a new perspective. Meet someone new and listen to their story. If you drink coffee every day, try tea tomorrow. Whenever we are facing change, if we can embrace it in small ways, it will become easier to embrace it in big ways.

5) **Create a new (good) habit.** In times of change, we can feel out of control. Create a sense of focus and control in a positive way by forming a new habit. Maybe, you've been wanting to drink more water for years - now is a great time to build that into your life. Maybe, you know you need to get more exercise – add three afternoon walks per week to your routine. The mental discipline of forming a new habit will create momentum and the sense of accomplishment will empower you. Always start with a small habit to ensure you will be successful.

CHAPTER NINE
Embracing Change:
Mack's Perspective

MACK'S THOUGHTS

"All meaningful and lasting change starts first in your imagination and then works its way out."

~ Albert Einstein

What can you imagine? Can you see yourself embracing change as a valuable way of supercharging your career? Can you see yourself less stressed out about change? Can you see yourself seeking change intentionally as a way to grow? Can you see leaders seeking your input?

When it comes to embracing change, there's a magic word you can proactively use to begin separating yourself from the crowd in a way that allows you to get noticed by the high impact leaders and promoted for the right reasons. The magic word is "HOW?" Before I tell you how to use the magic word, I want to share a few thoughts with you.

Fear of change will create self-doubt if you choose to be reactive instead of proactive. When you choose to be reactive, you begin to look for the negative impact the change will have on you, whether it's at work or at home. *Reactive* people quickly become the *victim* of change.

As you begin to think of all the different ways change is going to negatively impact you, your imagination begins to run wild in the *wrong* direction. When this happens, you are no longer in control. You're out of control and along for the ride.

However, when you embrace change, you are also embracing responsibility. When you embrace responsibility, you are being proactive. This is where the magic word truly becomes magical. When change happens, proactive people do not immediately begin to ask, "What's going to happen?" They pull out their magic word: HOW?

Listen to the voices of those proactively embracing change:

- *How* would a proactive person respond?
- *How* will I be viewed if I respond positively?
- *How* can I help others embrace the change?
- *How* will this benefit me?
- *How* can I leverage this change to my benefit?
- *How* will this benefit our team?
- *How* will this benefit the organization?
- *How* will this make us more competitive?
- *How* can I help make it happen?

I captured this quote while reading one of Ria's books. She said, *"If we embrace the chance of living life to the fullest, then we must be willing to accept responsibility for doing it."* If we're going to embrace change and become responsible for leading ourselves and others through change effectively, we must be willing to use the magic word: HOW?

When you ask, *"How* can I?" or *"How* can we?" instead of "Can I?" or "Can we?" you have started to truly transform the way you and others think. "Can I?" indicates self-doubt. You don't know if you can. But, when you say *"How* can I?" you have already decided you will and you can. Therefore, your imagination can run wild in the *right* direction.

"How can I?" indicates there is a way. You just need to discover it. Asking *how* triggers the proactive muscles in your mind, and you get busy trying to find a way. You'll discover there's often more than one way. Proactive people are very creative. Reactive people are very stuck. Stuck playing the role of victim.

Once you choose to embrace change, you are positioned to begin leveraging change for your benefit. Michael F. Sciortino, Sr. shared these related proactive thoughts when he said, *"It really is amazing what happens when you recognize the importance of the opportunities ahead of you, accept responsibility for your future, and take positive action."*

How can you do that? *How* can you *begin* to recognize the importance of change? *How* can you *accept* responsibility for change? And most importantly, *how* can you take *positive* action when change happens? *How* can you *leverage* change to your benefit?

Not too long ago, I was conducting numerous half day onsite leadership development sessions for a company. Some people were resistant, reactive, and negative. Most were open and receptive. And, a few were gung ho!

Those are the ones who fire me up. It's like they're sitting in the audience with a big "HOW?" sign flashing over their head. They are engaged and trying to figure out *how* they can benefit from what I'm teaching and sharing.

While most in the company were basically neutral at best or negative at worst, there were two who embraced it. They multiplied what I was teaching them by proactively reading and growing beyond what was required by their employer. One of them initiated change, moved across the country, and more than doubled his pay. The other set out on a path to recapture his childhood dream of becoming a pro golfer. Both are doing well and making things happen.

For the others, very little has changed. Some made small improvements and received small benefits. But the two who truly embraced and leveraged change have launched like rockets. In the words of Samuel L. Parker, *"With awareness comes responsibility... responsibility to act."*

CHAPTER TEN
Leveraging Change:
Ria's Perspective

RIA'S THOUGHTS

"I cannot say whether things will get better if we change; what I can say is they must change if they are to get better."

~ Georg Lichtenburg

Leverage (the verb) is defined as "using a quality or advantage to obtain a desired result."

When we leverage something, we take advantage of the lever to multiply the results of our efforts. Leveraging something can be a powerful way to gain momentum and accelerate progress. But, we seldom think of change as something we can, or should, leverage.

Change always brings opportunities. When we leverage change we not only take advantage of the obvious opportunities, we create new ones as well. In order to leverage change and take advantage of or create opportunities, we first must see them. Then, we must be willing to put forth the effort to maximize them.

All of us have formed habits, usually in a physical or mental area of our life, that haven't served us as well as we would like. Perhaps, it's a mid-afternoon cookies and milk habit that has caused you to pack on a few pounds. Perhaps, it's a check your phone every time it buzzes, rings, or beeps habit that keeps you glued to the screen, even through conversations with your spouse. Perhaps, it's an addictive TV habit that has "stolen" all your personal growth and reading time.

Whatever it is, you know it's not a good habit and doesn't really serve your goals and values, yet cutting down or cutting out a bad habit isn't easy. You may have tried to cut out all the cookies from your diet only to find yourself caving in late afternoon to that chocolaty crunch. You think it helps with that afternoon slump while working at your desk.

Then, your boss decides to schedule a daily team huddle – every afternoon during your "cookie break." The change in routine brings some disruption to your schedule – but, it also brings the opportunity to change up or eliminate your cookie habit.

The temptation may be to simply work around the obstacle – cookies can happen before or after the team huddle – but instead, you can leverage the change in routine to form a healthier snack habit. Or, better yet, eliminate it all together.

Mack and I went to Guatemala a few years ago with a team of coaches to train Guatemalan leaders on leadership principles. We wanted to maximize our experience of "being there" and also avoid expensive data charges, so we decided not to use our cell phones while we were there. We were there for an entire week, and it was amazing how I found myself reaching for my phone often to check emails, post a status update, or check in to my ever present calendar.

By the end of the week however, the urge to have my phone constantly in my hand had faded.

The change in my routine for a week brought about an unexpected opportunity for me to change my phone habits. I now check the phone when I am ready – and I've learned I don't have to check it every time it beeps, buzzes, chirps, or tweets. Just because it rings doesn't mean I have to stop a conversation to answer it. It's been incredibly freeing to have more control over that area of my life, but I probably wouldn't have made the change if I had not been able to leverage a change in my routine for several days.

Anytime we are experiencing change, we can learn to leverage it by looking for the opportunities.

Ask yourself these six questions:

1) What does this change mean for me personally?

2) What areas of my life does this change impact? (social/relational, mental/emotional, physical, or spiritual)

3) How does this affect my environment?

4) What opportunities does this change bring?

5) How can I create more opportunities from this change?

6) How can I leverage this change to make a bigger improvement with this opportunity?

When you find yourself stressed out over a change, it's especially important to spend time reflecting on how to leverage it. Change brings disruption. Disruption can be positive just as it can be negative.

The bigger the change is, the bigger the disruption will be, and the bigger the opportunities will be when you learn to look for them and leverage them. Change cracks open a door. To leverage change, you must push it all the way open and walk through it.

CHAPTER TEN
Leveraging Change:
Mack's Perspective

MACK'S THOUGHTS

"A sign of wisdom and maturity is when you come to terms with the realization that your decisions cause your rewards and consequences. You are responsible for your life, and your ultimate success depends on the choices you make."

~ Denis Waitley

Once you've made the choice to embrace change, don't stop there. Leverage the change for maximum benefit. Leveraging change means doing more than simply making the change. Leveraging change means you will seek ways to intentionally *grow your influence* during the change.

You will benefit greatly by simply embracing change and choosing not to resist. When you move from resisting change to embracing change, you move from being viewed as reactive to being viewed as neutral. But, if you choose to *leverage the change*, you will move from being viewed as neutral to being viewed as proactive.

When it comes to change, who will have the most influence with their leader? Someone who is reactive, neutral, or proactive? No doubt, the proactive person will have the most influence. As you begin leveraging change, there will be many benefits that will help you grow and advance your career professionally.

7 Benefits of Leveraging Change in the Workplace

1) **You will be noticed for taking initiative.** The first to help always gets the most recognition. Quickly implement change and be sure to suggest change that will benefit the process, team, or business in some way.

2) **You will build strong relationships with the game changers.** When you embrace change, you are attracting others who embrace and initiate change. The best advertisement is *word of mouth* advertisement. What are your co-workers and leaders saying about your business (YOU)?

3) **You will get to learn more about how the business operates.** As you interact with more game changers, you will build trust. Be sure to ask questions to learn the thought process behind the change. This will most likely increase your influence in the future.

4) **You will have more input in implementing the change.** When you get involved with making the change happen, you will be given a voice. You will be asked your opinion, and others will learn how you think.

5) **You will have more input in future changes.** As you build relationships and interact with leaders during change, they will begin asking your opinion about future changes. At this point, you're gaining valuable influence.

6) **You will become more valuable.** When leaders start to benefit from your support and your ideas for improving the processes and moving the organization forward, you become more valuable to them and the organization.

7) **You will be considered for promotions.** Those who make an impact helping the leaders implement change will be more quickly considered for pay increases and promotions because of the strong supportive relationship they have built with the decision makers.

As you begin to realize these and other benefits, you will have leveraged change. Those who are neutral or resistant will never receive these benefits. As you already know, most people don't like change and put their energy into resisting and complaining. *When others are moaning, groaning, and whining, it's easy for you to start shining.*

When you choose to be proactive when everyone else is being reactive, that mindset is already allowing you to leverage change to your benefit. Look for those opportunities when there is a change. Be the first to support the leader not only privately, but also publicly.

Loyalty publicly leads to leverage privately. This is another way to intentionally leverage change for your benefit. When you support those responsible for change openly, in a way they know you are behind them, you will increase your influence with them when you meet with them privately, perhaps to recommend a change of your own.

When you leverage change, you're essentially building trust. The more trust you have with the leaders, the more influence you'll have with them. As Amy Cuddy says, *"If someone you're trying to influence doesn't trust you, you're not going to get very far; in fact, you might even elicit suspicion because you come across as manipulative."*

When you're leading (influencing) others, your goal should be to motivate, not manipulate. When you are motivating, all parties benefit. When you are manipulating, only you benefit. Therefore, as you begin to leverage change for your benefit, you must do it in a way that allows the leaders to benefit. And, if possible, those on your team. When more people benefit from your actions, you will gain more influence.

The ultimate test of a leader is to produce positive change. *Leading change leverages change.* Are you ready?

CHAPTER ELEVEN
Leading Change:
Ria's Perspective

RIA'S THOUGHTS

"Intelligence is the ability to adapt to change."

~ Stephen Hawking

When we talk about leading change, it's important to remember the most difficult, and most important, person to lead is oneself. We must lead within before we can lead without.

Leadership is influence – and typically, we think of influence in terms of influencing someone else: spouse, children, co-workers, boss, friend, or family member. Or maybe, you want to "influence" the salesman to give you a better deal. Regardless of who else you are trying to influence (lead), we seldom think of leadership and influence as something we can and should do for ourselves.

We can influence our thoughts, feelings, emotions and that will lead to influence over our actions, words, and deeds. James Allen said, *"A man's mind may be likened to a garden, which may be intelligently cultivated or allowed to run wild; but whether cultivated or neglected, it must, and will, bring forth. If no useful seeds are put into it, then an abundance of useless weed seeds will fall therein, and will continue to produce their kind."*

Have you ever been driving down the road upset or angry about something and decided to turn the radio on? Suddenly, one of your favorite songs comes on. Your finger starts tapping on the wheel. You start humming a little. And, just that quick, your bad mood has evaporated.

Or, perhaps for you, it's a shopping trip (I call it "Retail Therapy") and a new pair of shoes will pick you up in a heartbeat. Nearly everyone has a few things they can do when they are feeling down, upset, or angry, that helps lift them back up. But, it's not the song or the shoes (or whatever) that have magic. It's what you tell yourself about whatever it is you are doing that picks you back up. It helps when you put things in perspective and tell yourself it isn't so bad after all.

If we can influence our thoughts some of the time, why not do it all of the time?

This concept is simple. The idea we can influence our thoughts, feelings, and therefore our actions, means we don't have to be subject to our external environment. We don't have to be like a ship being tossed about on the sea of life. However, as is often the case, simple to understand doesn't mean easy to do.

The greatest gap in life is the gap between knowing and doing. When we know what we should do and don't follow through, we are *destroying* our personal integrity. When we know what we should do and follow through, we *build* our personal integrity and also credibility with other people, thus making it easier to influence self and others in the future.

Here are three ways to influence and lead change within yourself by making conscious choices when you consider:

1) **What you think about.** Leading change with oneself begins by choosing your thoughts carefully. The moment you feel negative about the changes, stop and think about the benefits or positive aspects of the situation. Oprah Winfrey said, *"What you focus on expands,"* and that's especially true for situations where you are dealing with change. Focus on the negatives, and they will magnify until they overwhelm you. Focus on the positives, and you will find more of them.

2) **What you tell yourself.** You are the most important person you will ever talk to. Because, whatever you tell yourself carries far more weight in terms of impact on your mental state. You can talk yourself into or out of just about anything. Embrace change by looking at the situation honestly and evaluating how you are talking to yourself about the change. Are you telling yourself it was better the old way? If so, you will never embrace the changes or lead others through them. Tell yourself you are moving on. *Times change, and so should you.*

3) **What you tell others.** It's almost as if speaking something out loud affirms it and makes it *feel* true. The more we repeat something to someone else, the more we believe it too – until we know it's true without a doubt. Your words carry weight. That's why focusing on the positive is so important.

Our minds are incredibly powerful tools and should be used wisely. Be careful to lead yourself well in times of change, and that will help you lead others well. You can spend time and energy blaming everyone else for having to change – but at the end of the day, that doesn't mean you won't have to deal with it anyway.

Make it a point to lead yourself well relative to dealing with change by staying positive, guarding your thoughts, and considering what you tell yourself and everyone else.

CHAPTER ELEVEN
Leading Change:
Mack's Perspective

MACK'S THOUGHTS

"While one person hesitates because he feels inferior, another person is making mistakes, and becoming superior."

~ Henry C. Link

Don't let the fear of change stop you from becoming a high impact leader of change. There's more potential in you. Once you've mastered applying what Ria and I have covered already, you're ready to climb your way farther up the leadership mountain. The higher you climb, the better it gets because you'll find much greater rewards along the path. You'll begin to impact lives instead of processes.

Since leadership is defined as influence, you don't need a formal leadership position to do the things you're learning throughout this book. You simply need a desire to leverage your influence by applying the principles. If you have a position, great. If you don't, keep leading change, and it'll only be a matter of time before you're offered one.

As I write the remaining chapters, I'm going to assume you've mastered proactively embracing, supporting, and leveraging change. If you truly have, you should be proud. You are far ahead of the pack at this point and have separated yourself from the masses, the reactive people who will forever remain average, and often miserable, as they struggle through life...*unless they choose to change.*

Once you're able to effectively lead yourself through change using the principles we've been sharing, you will be prepared to begin intentionally leading others through change. Because you have experienced the growth and transformation yourself, you'll be perfectly positioned to *see how others see, feel what others feel,* and help them learn *how* to embrace change.

Actually, you can use this book as a training manual as you engage and lead others through change. With 30, three page sections, you can easily use it to conduct a 30 day book study with your family, friends, co-workers, or team members. So, mark it up, make it your own, but *don't* give it away. It's a valuable tool and a resource you will want to keep, especially if you marked it up and made it your own.

While you're helping others overcome the challenge of change, you will be simultaneously climbing the corporate ladder and pay scale. It's a win-win. They win because you are helping them win just as Ria and I are helping you win. But, you will also win because you'll be gaining 360° influence as you prove yourself to be a leader worth following.

Some people don't have a desire to climb the corporate ladder; however, most do want to climb the pay scale. If you're not interested in bigger and better positions, your goal should be to be the best at what you do, where you're doing it. You can simply enjoy work with much less stress and continue to lead change from wherever you are without the worries of the additional formal responsibility that comes with climbing the corporate ladder.

You will have the option to lead yourself and others from where you are now, or you'll have the option to become an even more effective and intentional leader of change. When you learn to effectively lead change, your influence will grow, and you will have many more options. Options you can't even begin to imagine today.

As you continue to develop influence, it will only be a matter of time before it is recognized. High impact leaders will begin to encourage, engage, and empower you. You'll be given additional opportunities to prove yourself. Then, at some point, you'll be offered a formal leadership position if you don't have one or a higher level leadership position if you do.

Getting results is the quickest way to build trust. Therefore, when you can implement change effectively in support of the leaders in a way that helps them accomplish their mission, they will begin to figure out where you can make a bigger impact and how they can better position and utilize you.

What are the leaders doing? Exactly what you learned about in the last chapter, *leveraging change*.

When they can change your role and give you more authority and responsibility for making changes, not only will they and the organization benefit, you will also benefit. Remember, change is your friend. Becoming a high impact leader is simply another progressive change that will allow you to realize and benefit from the potential someone sees inside you. Jim Rohn made this very relative point, *"Life does not get better by chance. It gets better by change."*

I'm encouraging you to grow to the next level and beyond. Once you see the many benefits of change, you can become what is often referred to as change agent or champion of change on a very intentional mission to make things happen within your department, organization, or life. How high will you climb?

Everything you ever achieve will be a direct result of your ability to influence (lead) other people.

CHAPTER TWELVE
Communicating Change:
Ria's Perspective

RIA'S THOUGHTS

"Education is the most powerful weapon which you can use to change the world."

~ Nelson Mandela

I left home at 19 without a job, a car, or a high school diploma. I left an abusive home life where I grew up very isolated from "normal" society, and I didn't learn to communicate very well. I would barely talk to people at all.

My first job was working as a server at a pizza restaurant. I worked the lunch shift, Monday through Friday every day, from 11:00 – 2:00. Most customers would have the all-you-can-eat pizza and salad buffet, because it was fast and cheap.

I was the only lunch server for all 36 tables in the restaurant. My job was to set up the buffet, keep the salad bar stocked and clean, make the tea, fill the ice bin, stock the soda machine, answer the phone, take delivery orders, greet the customers when they entered, take and fill their drink orders, keep dirty plates bussed, refill their drinks, check them out at the cash register, clean the tables, chairs, and floor after the customer left, wash all the dishes, put them away, and restock everything before I left. All for $2.13 per hour, plus any tips I made.

The lunch buffet was $5.99, and a drink was $1.35. So, most customer bills came to less than $8.00 for lunch. The average tip is 10% for a buffet, so the best tip I could expect would be about $1.00 – if I hustled really hard to keep their soda refilled and the dirty plates bussed. If I got too busy and the customer ran out of tea, I wouldn't get a tip at all.

I learned quickly that being an "introverted" waitress

who didn't communicate wasn't going to work. If I didn't smile at the customers, they thought I was unfriendly. If I didn't greet them enthusiastically, they didn't feel welcome or appreciated as customers. If I didn't remember the names of the regular customers and what they liked to drink, they wouldn't even leave me the change from their dollar.

I learned a lot of things during my years of waiting tables off and on throughout the early days of my career. You see the best and the worst of people when you wait tables. The most important lesson I learned was this: I needed to take initiative and communicate with my customers.

It was a lesson that stuck with me. I could tell them where to get a plate and take their drink order, but how I did it made all the difference in whether they left me anything at all, or sometimes, several dollars.

Communicating is one of the *critical* success skills in life, but communication during *change* is even more imperative.

How and what we choose to communicate about change, either at work or at home, determines if we build trust with everyone around us. Being open and transparent in your communication builds trust, while hoarding information about what's going on creates distrust.

Even if you don't have all the answers, it's important to communicate what you do know. I remember when I resigned from my job as director at the hospital. It was a delicate time. I needed to be transparent and communicate the changes, with the right people, at the right time.

My vice-president was the first person to know, and I told my team members immediately afterward. I knew their first question would be, "How will this impact our department?"

I couldn't answer that right away. I knew it was important to let them know about the changes as soon as possible, so they didn't hear about it from someone else first. That built trust. I also was very up front with them. I didn't know exactly how the transition and my resignation would work, but I gave them all the information I could to help reassure them.

Then, as we mapped a plan for my transition out of the organization, I communicated to them directly as soon as possible. And, I made sure to communicate with them all equally – no one got "the scoop" before anyone else because I knew that would damage their relationships.

It was a huge time of change. They all had to change offices, they got a new leader, and they had to change up roles to absorb some of my work.

18 weeks later, I walked out of my office for the last time and felt good about it. The department had made the change with as few bumps as possible.

The greater the change, the greater the need for communication. Quick and timely communication of accurate information can make or break you when things are changing fast. Think of the need for communication between a team of paramedics. There isn't time for any of them to hold back important information – because someone's life is at stake. If we take just as much priority in communicating changes in our own roles at work and at home, we will be much more successful in times of change and crisis. Open communication is critical. If communication fails, so will you.

CHAPTER TWELVE
Communicating Change:
Mack's Perspective

MACK'S THOUGHTS

"The most important thing in communication is to hear what isn't being said."

~ Peter Drucker

As a leader (influencer) of change, your #1 goal is to get buy-in from those who will be affected by the change and/or responsible for implementing the change. Without buy-in, everything else becomes much more complicated. People always buy-in to the leader before they buy-in to the leader's vision. You are the key to your own success.

You must keep in mind, *leadership is influence.* It's not about authority or formal position. However, if you do have a position of authority, it's even *more critical* that you lay your power and authority aside and choose to lead with moral authority, *influence.* When a leader has to use an iron fist to implement change, trouble is on the horizon.

One of the most powerful ways to get buy-in is to insure others feel understood before you try to be understood. Let them go first. When faced with change from above, would you prefer to be told what's changing and told how to deal with it? Or, would you prefer to be involved from the start? Most, would say, "I want to be involved."

When you allow others to be involved with making changes on the front end, things go much smoother on the backend. Sharing information with those who will be affected by the change builds trust and increases buy-in by giving them a voice to express concerns and to make suggestions. Leaders understand none of us is as smart as all of us. None of us is as creative as all of us. And, none of us has as much experience as all of us.

Liz Wiseman was on target when she suggested, *"The critical skill of this century is not what you hold in your head, but your ability to tap into and access what other people know. The best leaders and the fastest learners know how to harness collective intelligence."* Her words ring true. High impact leaders unleash their team's potential by taking the complex and making it simple. The key is to listen with your eyes and ears for feelings.

Change often creates emotional responses. Many people get mad, sad, frustrated, fearful, and anxious when change happens. Most of these emotions are based in the unknown. When people don't know, they start wondering and guessing. Then, they start comparing their guesses with other's guesses in an attempt to create fact. Next, they start spreading their guesses, which have now been converted into "fact," throughout the organization. This is also known as spreading rumors.

A high impact leader will proactively prevent rumors on the front end by engaging those affected by the change. Leaders ask questions to uncover feelings. Kevin Cashman observed, *"Authentic listening is not easy. We hear the words, but rarely do we really slow down to listen and squint with our ears to hear the emotions, fears, and underlying concerns."*

As a high impact leader, when it comes to change, you're like a parent standing in a pool trying to get your toddler to jump in with you. Unless the toddler trusts you, it's not going to happen. However, the parent's past behavior will be key. Likewise, when you're leading change, the amount of trust you've built up in advance will determine much, if not all, of your success.

If they trust you in advance, they are included from the start, and they are approached with the intent to be understood, you will have a much better chance at success. It will take a little more time on the front end.

But, it will save you a lot of time and headaches on the backend. Pat Parelli stated it simply when he said, *"Take the time it takes, so it takes less time."*

If you run into resistance, *answer questions with questions.* It's always easier to lead with questions instead of directions. By asking a question, you are transferring the responsibility of finding a solution to the team member. The interesting thing is one or both of you will learn something from the questions. And ultimately, you will agree on the solution. That's buy-in. Don't listen to the answers with the intent to reply. Listen with the intent to understand. Once they feel understood, they will be much more open to listening to you.

Imagine you went into the doctor's office because you were not feeling well. The doctor walks in, says hello, writes you a prescription, says you'll be better soon, and walks out the door. You would have no confidence in the doctor's prescription until you felt he understood you and your symptoms. Then, you would be happy to listen and follow his recommendations.

It's much the same in the workplace. Leaders of change must understand and apply the principle of seeking to genuinely understand those who will be affected by the change. If you're the leader, you have the right to speak. However, you must earn the right to be heard.

You will decide when you will speak and what you will say. But, the team members will only listen if they have bought-in. Without buy-in, they will only do what they have to do. With buy-in, they will do what they have to do *plus* what they *want* to do.

CHAPTER THIRTEEN
Initiating Change:
Ria's Perspective

RIA'S THOUGHTS

"The pessimist complains about the wind; the optimist expects it to change; the realist adjusts the sails."

~ William Arthur Ward

When you initiate change, you take responsibility. Initiating change requires a proactive approach and only proactive people will do it. Initiating change requires you to say "I will" instead of "I wish."

Change is never easy. Whether we are changing the culture of an organization or our eating habits, to initiate and create change, we must choose to act.

Initiating change requires a higher level of emotional intelligence. Only those who are very proactive will take the initiative to make change happen because they must buy-in to the "why" of the change enough to overcome the resistance that will certainly surface.

When you initiate change, you are telling the world you are not willing to settle for average. You are saying you are not willing to settle for the "status quo."

"Status quo" is a myth anyway – nothing stays the same in life. You are either going forward and making progress or going backward. George Bernard Shaw said, *"Progress is impossible without change, and those who cannot change their minds cannot change anything."*

Moving from passive to proactive requires a strong connection to the values driving the need for change. For example, let's say you eat lunch out every Friday to treat yourself going into the weekend. You treat yourself to a hamburger, french-fries and a milkshake. However, you've noticed your Friday lunch habit has caused you to pack on a few extra pounds. So, you decide to have a salad this Friday instead.

You are being proactive when you decide to have the salad. However, you must continue to be proactive all the way through ordering and consuming your meal, or you will simply regress back to passive.

When you regress back to passive, you will justify your decision to yourself. "I've had a stressful week, and I need a treat." You tell yourself as you contemplate that chocolaty milkshake, "I'll eat healthy this weekend and make up for it." You bargain with yourself in an attempt to rationalize your decision.

When we initiate change within ourselves, we must be bought-in to a big enough "why." That means, when you place your order on Friday at lunch and contemplate the salad instead of your usual Friday treat, you also consider "why" you wanted the salad to begin with. You are making your decision based on your values of eating healthier. If you aren't bought-in to the "why," then it will be all too easy to fall back to temptation.

When we initiate change in others, we must be able to help them see and understand the "why," so we can help them embrace the change.

As a coach, I've found the best way I can do that is to ask questions around the benefits of change. It's not enough for the client to know they want to change. They must understand from within "why" they want to change. Once we know "why" we want to change, we have the fuel to propel us through the change.

As you contemplate initiating change, it can be overwhelming. The key to success, after you have identified the "why," is to break it down into smaller steps. As Lao Tzu said, *The journey of a thousand miles begins with a single step.*

Then, instead of looking at all of the steps you need to take, just focus on the first one or the most important.

Focus on the one thing you need to do, that if it doesn't happen, the rest of the steps don't matter.

What I love about initiating change is actually making something happen. Causing something to improve for the better isn't easy – but it's certainly rewarding! There is something to be said about the hormone dopamine and your body's physiological response to setting and accomplishing a goal. It makes us feel good, and we want to do it again, and again. Learn to leverage that on the front end to initiate change by starting with small changes when necessary. Small changes can be extremely powerful, especially when compounded over time.

Big changes might be more difficult to implement, but the momentum in making a large change successfully can be huge, helping you build up enough steam to tackle other big changes.

Large or small, the most important thing is to get started. Once you have had a little success, it will be easier to continue. But, don't stop to celebrate your initial success too long. You will lose the momentum you built up. Then, you must start over again. It's much harder to get started than it is to keep going.

Initiating change can be like pushing a giant boulder up a big hill. You must put more energy into the first step. If you don't keep pushing, the boulder will roll back. If you must start again, you won't have as much energy as you did for the first push. It will be even more difficult on a second or third attempt. That's why we must keep going once we start something. If the change is worth starting, then it's worth following through with.

CHAPTER THIRTEEN
Initiating Change:
Mack's Perspective

MACK'S THOUGHTS

"Responsibility and roles are not something that must be handed down; they are taken as one assumes more and more responsibility in the organization."

~ Jimmy Collins

If you want to get to the next level in any area of life, you must be proactive. You shouldn't always wait to be given responsibility from a leader above before you act. You should *take responsibility* and do what needs to be done because it needs to be done, not because it's your job to get it done. As you take more responsibility, your influence will grow.

Relative to change, the responsibility you need to *take* is in the area of initiating and leading change. The most valuable team members intentionally solve problems and improve processes. Find something that needs to be fixed or improved, determine what needs to be changed, and initiate the change. I often speak about the three different levels of initiation.

3 Levels of Change Initiation

1) **Identify a problem.** At level 1, you take responsibility for identifying problems, but you expect someone else to be responsible for solving them. You are communicating to the leader you don't want to take responsibility, and you're unwilling to think for yourself. In this case, *you are part of the problem, not part of the solution.* All you do is inform the leader you have discovered a problem. Then, the leader determines what needs to be changed to solve the problem.

2) **Identify a problem, and provide a solution.** At level 2, you take responsibility for identifying a solution to an identified problem before you notify the leader. You want the leader to learn how you think and to have confidence in you. Basically, you tell the leader, "I've identified a problem, and I'd like to propose the following change to solve the problem." You're responsible for thinking about a solution before you get the leader involved. You're simply seeking agreement and approval to implement your change. The leader will notice your desire to take more responsibility. The leader will respect, value, and trust you more. Your influence with the leader will increase.

3) **Identify a problem, and solve the problem.** Once you've earned trust with your leader at level 2, you're ready to move on to level 3. In this case, you have discovered an opportunity to solve a problem. You have worked alone or with your team, to develop a solution for the problem. You have also implemented the solution and validated it. The problem is solved. When you see the leader, you simply say, "I identified a problem, and this is what I/we did to solve it." At level 3, the leader trusts you. You are now a *part of the solution* and no longer a part of the problem.

What do you do if everything seems to be fine? You look for something to improve. When change happens, you must respond to the change. However, when you're leading and initiating change, you and/or your team are looking for something to change. I'm reminded of the words of Will Rogers, *"Even if you are on the right track, you'll get run over if you just sit there."*

Organizations and people that choose to sit still will be passed by those who are initiating positive change to improve processes and solve problems. When you are intentionally initiating change, there are many different types of opportunities to consider: something isn't working right, something is frustrating, a process is slow, quality issues or mistakes often occur, there are safety concerns, etc.

In the past, when I was leading the lean manufacturing kaizen (continuous improvement) teams, everything we did was related to initiating change. We were proactively seeking to increase productivity, reduce changeover or setup times, reduce lead-times, organize and standardize areas to improve safety and productivity, reduce machine downtime due to maintenance issues, improve on-time shipments, reduce costs, etc.

When you want to lead change and intentionally improve processes, you will find endless opportunities to initiate change. To continuously grow yourself and advance your career, don't focus on becoming more successful, *focus on becoming more valuable.* When leaders see you initiating change, improving processes, and getting results with and through others, you will get noticed and become a more valuable team player.

James Allen had this to say about getting results, *"We are anxious to improve our circumstances but unwilling to improve ourselves. We therefore remain bound."* If you truly want to initiate a change that will redirect your life and unleash your potential, focus on changing yourself.

CHAPTER FOURTEEN
Become a Change Champion:
Ria's Perspective

RIA'S THOUGHTS

"Failure is not fatal, but failure to change might be."

~ John Wooden

A study of history shows us innumerable examples of companies, organizations, churches, and even countries that did not change and ultimately failed.

One example is Blockbuster, a video rental company. The interesting thing is Blockbuster made the transition from the old VHS tapes to the new DVD technology without a hitch. They responded to the change in technology and kept right on going. Then, video streaming technology appeared on the scene and companies like Netflix put them out of business fast.

Consider how failure to change can impact us on a personal level as well. The vast majority of business professionals today must be able to operate a computer, navigate the internet, and respond to email. Many job applications are now online only. For students today, knowing their multiplication table is important, but knowing how to use a laptop is more important.

For highly successful people, or those who want to become highly successful, it's not enough simply to change when forced to. Highly successful people realize they must become a change champion – seeking change and helping others do the same. They must see, value, and act on the need for change in order to be successful.

In order to be a change champion, you must learn to lead others. This starts by leading yourself. But, it doesn't stop there.

Here are seven ways you can build your influence and leadership with others in order to become a *Change Champion*:

1) **Do more than expected.** Go above and beyond, whether it's at work or at home. At work, when someone asked me to research a Medicare regulation, I found the regulation online and sent it to them. But, I also took the time to read the regulation, tell them what it meant to them and how it impacted them, and then sent them a summary with a source link to the original document. I also highlighted and summarized the important information for easy reference. Yes, it took more of my time, but I quickly became the "go-to" person for help with regulations.

2) **Do it before it is required.** If you know something needs to be done – do it. Don't wait to be asked or "voluntold" because the first person to step up without being asked will be noticed as a leader long before the person who is asked to comply. Look around you for tasks that need to be done. Parents would love it if their kids did that. Your supervisor would love it if you did it. For that matter, your spouse would love it too. Vacuum or mow the lawn without being asked.

3) **Be confident and humble.** There is a fine line between confidence and arrogance – it's called humility. Don't be afraid to speak up when you know the answer to a question, but also don't be afraid to admit if you don't know something. Being humble enough to learn will take you a long way in any relationship.

4) **Admit mistakes.** We all make mistakes. It's simply a fact of life. We will experience failure and have an opportunity to learn from it. Admit it – and then act to correct it. Apologize (sincerely) when necessary. Fix it – and move on.

5) **Volunteer to help others.** It shouldn't have to be said, but it does. Those who have a heart for serving others in some way will build influence far beyond those who expect to be served. It doesn't always require a lot of effort – helping someone can be as little as opening a door for someone or as big as helping them move. It could be staying late to help a co-worker finish a project. Second mile doesn't have to be second rate.

6) **Take more responsibility.** When you take responsibility for making something happen, you own the situation. Asking *how* you can do something allows you to think through a solution, instead of asking *if* you can do something. Little words – big attitude change.

7) **Accept less credit, but more blame.** None of us accomplish much of anything alone. We all got to where we are today with the help of others at some point. Maybe, it was just a chance opportunity. Or, someone took a chance on you and gave you a job. Regardless, accept more of the blame when things go wrong and share more of the credit with others when things go right.

CHAPTER FOURTEEN
Become a Change Champion:
Mack's Perspective

MACK'S THOUGHTS

"Leadership education is not reserved for people with titles. We focus on people who want to take the next step in their leadership journey, no matter what their official title or role is."

~ Bob Chapman

High impact leaders make the best change champions because they value others, they believe in others, and they build strong relationships with others. They are constantly changing and investing in their own growth, as you are now, not only to improve themselves, but also to help improve others. It's not about the leader, but it starts with the leader.

If you're going to become a highly respected leader of change worth following, you must *change the way you believe in people.* They need to feel your belief in them, not just hear about it. If you have a leadership title, great. If you don't, great. *Leadership is about who you are, not what you are or where you sit.*

If you want to champion change, you must learn to lead people effectively. What makes someone a leader? When someone chooses to follow you because they want to, not because they have to, then you are a leader. It has nothing to do with power, authority, position, title, rank, age, years of experience, etc.

High impact leaders embrace Simon Sinek's words, *"Leadership is not a license to do less; it is a responsibility to do more."* One of the quickest ways to get someone to voluntarily follow you is to express total belief in them as a person in a way that unleashes their potential. That's the responsibility of a leader. If we only believe in people because we trust them, have faith in them, and have confidence in them, we are being selfish and judgmental.

There's a better, unselfish, non-judgmental way to believe in people. I watched a TEDx video recently and heard Joshua Encarnacion say, *"We need to change the way we believe in people. We need to move beyond trust, faith, and confidence. We need to shift to encouragement, empowerment, and engagement."* What a powerful lesson I received from him. He went on to say how encouraging, engaging, and empowering others doesn't require judgment and is selfless.

This is a principle. It applies everywhere and with all people. You can apply it at work with your co-workers, regardless of anyone's position or title. You can and should apply this at home with your family. If you've ever heard someone you care about say, "I *believed* in you." You know the hurt judgment can bring when you feel as though you let them down and have lost their trust, faith, and confidence forever.

When we're encouraging, empowering, and engaging others, they are allowed to make mistakes. We can still authentically believe in them because our belief is based in caring and valuing them as people regardless of their actions. I call this *unconditional belief.* I'm sure you understand the concept of unconditional love. It's exactly the same but based on belief in the other person, not caring for the other person. You do care about them, but you also believe in them *unconditionally.*

Encouraging others when change happens communicates things are going to get better. Encouraging others communicates you believe they can make the necessary adjustments. Encouraging others communicates you believe in their ability to deal with the changes going on around them.

Empowering others when change happens gives them a voice regarding the changes. Empowering others shows you believe in their ability to identify and solve problems. Empowering others allows them to become responsible for implementing the change.

Engaging others when change happens gets them involved with the process. Engaging others transfers the responsibility for results to them. Engaging others allows them to make a bigger difference.

When you change how you believe in others, you'll change how they believe in themselves. That's what leaders do. They make a difference in the lives they touch.

When change happens, high impact leaders leverage the change and seize the opportunity to lead those around them. Because they have developed themselves, they're able to help others grow through change instead of go through change.

The most important changes you'll ever make are found on the inside, not the outside. If you move beyond change and embrace transformation, your life will never be the same. The key to transforming yourself is non-stop, intentional growth for the rest of your life.

I really like what my friend, Amir Ghannad, had to say, *"Change starts with 'what is' and attempts to keep what is working intact and eliminate what is not, transformation simply starts with 'nothing' and is led by a vision of the whole as if it were to be created from scratch today. The former views today as an extension of yesterday and tries to make the most of what is. The latter sees today as the beginning of tomorrow and shapes today's circumstances as a solid foundation for what will be."*

When I discovered my first leadership book, I chose transformation. I started building a fresh new foundation based on what *could be* if I applied what I was learning. Everything has changed. I didn't just make my job better. I made my life better in ways I couldn't imagine. You can do the same. I believe in you. Do you believe in yourself?

CHAPTER FIFTEEN
The Courage to Change:
Ria's Perspective

RIA'S THOUGHTS

"Our deepest fear is not that we are inadequate. Our deepest fear is that we are powerful beyond measure. It is our light not our darkness that most frightens us. We ask ourselves, who am I to be brilliant, gorgeous, talented and fabulous? Actually, who are you not to be?

You are a child of God. Your playing small doesn't serve the world. There's nothing enlightened about shrinking so that other people won't feel insecure around you. We were born to make manifest the glory of God that is within us.

It's not just in some of us; it's in everyone. And as we let our own light shine, we unconsciously give other people permission to do the same.

As we are liberated from our own fear; our presence automatically liberates others."

~ Marianne Williamson

Marianne Williamson's words touch me because they resonate with truth. I believe we are born with the knowledge that we are children of God, created in His image and gifted with talents and the ability to be an example of His glory. And yet, somewhere along the way, most of us forget or lose that knowledge.

For a long time, I had to take small steps to build up the courage and confidence to quit "playing small" in my own life and start letting my light shine. It's taken courage to change. It takes courage to let your light shine.

Perhaps, you have looked at yourself every day in the mirror and don't really see a major change in your image from day to day. But, if you see a picture of yourself from five or 10 years ago, you realize you have changed over time. Small changes are more difficult to see day to day.

Change is a part of life, but most of us are much more comfortable with the gradual and slow changes that occur over time. As a rule, we don't really like the discomfort that comes with drastic, sudden changes, even positive ones.

Stephen R. Covey said, *"There are three constants in life... change, choice, and principles."*

If it doesn't challenge you, it won't change you. We all have the potential to do more and be more in life. The problem is, most of us just let life happen rather than living intentionally.

You have only to look at Facebook on Monday mornings to read all about the people who aren't happy going to work. None of us wanted to grow up and work at a job we don't like. Yet, most are content to do nothing about it because it's easier to go along with the flow of life.

We often avoid the challenges that come with creating intentional changes, even positive ones, because we prefer the routine, the "normal" state, and the familiar. It takes *courage* to create change. You see, major change isn't easy for most of us.

We like comfortable and familiar circumstances, knowing the environment around us or the people around us, and knowing pretty much what will happen tomorrow is what happened today. We like routine as a rule. Work Monday through Friday, enjoy some R&R on the weekends, the occasional vacation, and then back to normal. We can get very comfortable surrounding ourselves with other people who are achieving only "average" results, because it doesn't challenge us. If we are surrounding ourselves with average, there is no pressure to be more than average.

There are a few people who embrace change because they realize in order to get different results, they must do things differently. Even if it means being a little uncomfortable with change, it's necessary to move forward toward a goal. They know the status quo isn't serving them or taking them where they want to be in six months, a year, or a decade.

When we embrace the concept of creating the changes we want, we can create the life we want. Every one of us are exactly where we should be based on each of the choices and decisions we have made in the past. If we want to be somewhere different in 90 days, six months, or a year, then we must do things differently.

Nelson Mandela said, *"There is no passion to be found in playing small – in settling for a life that is less than the one you are capable of living."*

It's time to stop playing small and start realizing your potential - personally, professionally, mentally, and even physically. It's time to start living a life with passion because you embrace change as an opportunity for things to get better.

I'm giving you permission to let your light shine and start living the life you want. Have the courage to change in order to create the life you want and don't settle for an average life. You have the potential to rise far above average.

Shine on!

CHAPTER FIFTEEN
The Courage to Change:
Mack's Perspective

MACK'S THOUGHTS

"Life shrinks or expands in proportion to one's courage."

~ Anais Nin

Change has the power to launch you into a new career, a new relationship, a new city, and even a new way of thinking. *When you change what you do, you change what you get.* Saying *no* to the wrong things frees you up to say *yes* to the right things. What you say yes to shapes your future. Saying no to something old gives you the freedom to say yes to something new.

Without the courage to change, you will get left behind by those brave enough to take risks and fail their way to a better future. Failure isn't really the appropriate word to use. Failure is actually often misused. People use the word failure as an excuse not to try something. However, it's only failure if you quit and never try again.

As a baby, you fell endless times as you attempted to walk. Try. Fail. Try. Fail. Try. Fail. But, that's not really what happened. In the end, did you *fail to walk*, or did you *learn to walk*? You learned to walk like the rest of us.

What really happened was this. Try. Learn. Try. Learn. Try. Learn. Try. Succeed. Find something new to learn.

The rest of life *should* be the same way. It took courage then, and it'll take even more courage to try new things now. Why? Because when you were learning to walk, you received endless encouragement from everyone around you. And most often, when you would fall, someone would pick you up. Learning as an adult is a bit harder.

Things are different once you grow up. As an adult, you will mostly receive a lot of doubting questions and negative feedback from other adults. If babies could talk and understand each other, they would probably never learn to walk. Could you imagine what it would be like in the nursery listening to the babies talking?

- Why do you want to walk?
- Don't you think you might fall?
- I tried that once, and it didn't work.
- Have you considered what will happen if you do fall? I bet it will really hurt!
- I saw Danny try that last week. He fell, broke his nose, and cried for hours.
- Have you thought about what will happen once you get going? How will you stop?

I was having a little fun with you, but I'm sure you get the point. That's what adults do all day long. You've heard those voices. They try to talk other adults out of trying something new because they're afraid themselves. If you want to get to a new level, you've got to change how you invest your time and who you invest it with.

You need to be reading, watching videos, or listening to audios of people who are doing what you want to be doing or that have done what you want to do. Whatever you do, don't seek advice about your life and your future from anyone who has not been where you want to go.

They don't know how to get there, and they don't want to go. Why would you ever give them a right to veto your dream? You shouldn't. Don't do it!

When it comes to effectively and courageously leading yourself through change, I want to leave you with a few nuggets of wisdom I've learned along the way that have had a tremendous and positive impact on my journey.

Ask yourself this question constantly, "Will what I'm about to do move me in the right direction?" However, it only works if you know where you're going. So, figure that out first. Then, if the answer is *yes*, do it immediately. If the answer is *no*, don't do it all. Get it right, move forward. Get it wrong, slow down, stop, or go backward. You first make your choices. Then, your choices make you. Not sometime. Every time.

Next, figure out what you need to stop doing, and stop doing it. This will free up some time and resources. Then, consider what's working great, and keep doing it. Finally, figure out what you're not doing, but should be doing, and start doing it.

These last two paragraphs are filled with many changes that will transform your life and deliver amazing results *if* you're willing to *change how you think*, and then, *change what you do*.

If you won't invest in your own growth and development, why should anyone else?

Courage allows you to transform yourself from who you are today to who you want to become tomorrow.

Brian Tracy said it this way, *"There are two types of courage that you need:*

First, you need the courage to launch, and to take action, to take a leap of faith. You need the courage to go 'all-in' without any guarantee of success and with a high possibility of failure, at least in the short-term.

The second type of courage that you need is called 'courageous patience.' This is the ability to hang in there and continue working and fighting after you have gone all in and before you have yet seen any results or rewards. Many people can muster up the courage to take action toward a new goal, but when they see no immediate results they quickly lose heart and pull back to safety and security. They don't have staying power."

Change what needs to be changed, not what is easy to change. Make it happen or someone else will.

READ MORE BOOKS BY MACK AND RIA

Excerpt from

Defining Influence:
Increasing Your Influence
Increases Your Options, by Mack Story

In *Defining Influence*, I outline the foundational leadership principles and lessons we must learn in order to develop our character in a way that allows us to increase our influence with others. I also share many of my personal stories revealing how I got it wrong many times in the past and how I grew from front-line factory worker to become a Motivational Leadership Speaker.

INTRODUCTION

When You Increase Your Influence, You Increase Your Options.

"Leadership is influence. Nothing more. Nothing less. Everything rises and falls on leadership." ~ John C. Maxwell

Everyone is born a leader. However, everyone is not born a high impact leader.

I haven't always believed everyone is a leader. You may or may not at this point. That's okay. There is a lot to learn about leadership.

At this very moment, you may already be thinking to yourself, *"I'm not a leader."* My goal is to help you understand why everyone is a leader and to help you develop a deeper understanding of the principles of leadership and influence.

Developing a deep understanding of leadership has

changed my life for the better. It has also changed the lives of my family members, friends, associates, and clients. My intention is to help you improve not only your life, but also the lives of those around you.

Until I became a student of leadership in 2008 which eventually led me to become a John Maxwell Certified Leadership Coach, Trainer, and Speaker in 2012, I did not understand leadership or realize everyone can benefit from learning the related principles.

In the past, I thought leadership was a term associated with being the boss and having formal authority over others. Those people are definitely leaders. But, I had been missing something. All of the other seven billion people on the planet are leaders too.

I say everyone is born a leader because I agree with John Maxwell, *"Leadership is Influence. Nothing more. Nothing less."* Everyone has influence. It's a fact. Therefore, everyone is a leader.

No matter your age, gender, religion, race, nationality, location, or position, everyone has influence. Whether you want to be a leader or not, you are. After reading this book, I hope you do not question whether or not you are a leader. However, I do hope you question what type of leader you are and what you need to do to increase your influence.

Everyone does not have authority, but everyone does have influence. There are plenty of examples in the world of people without authority leading people through influence alone. Actually, every one of us is an example. We have already done it. We know it is true. This principle is self-evident which means it contains its own evidence and does not need to be demonstrated or explained; it is obvious to everyone: we all have influence with others.

As I mentioned, the question to ask yourself is not, *"Am I a leader?"* The question to ask yourself is, *"What type of leader am I?"* The answer: whatever kind you choose to be. Choosing not to be a leader is not an option. As long as you live, you will have influence. You are a leader.

You started influencing your parents before you were actually born. You may have influence after your death. How? Thomas Edison still influences the world every time a light is turned on, you may do things in your life to influence others long after you're gone. Or, you may pass away with few people noticing. It depends on the choices you make.

Even when you're alone, you have influence.

The most important person you will ever influence is yourself. The degree to which you influence yourself determines the level of influence you ultimately have with others. Typically, when we are talking about leading ourselves, the word most commonly used to describe self-leadership is discipline which can be defined as giving yourself a command and following through with it. We must practice discipline daily to increase our influence with others.

"We must all suffer one of two things: the pain of discipline or the pain of regret or disappointment." ~ Jim Rohn

As I define leadership as influence, keep in mind the words leadership and influence can be interchanged anytime and anywhere. They are one and the same. Throughout this book, I'll help you remember by placing one of the words in parentheses next to the other occasionally as a reminder. They are synonyms. When you read one, think of the other.

Everything rises and falls on influence (leadership).

When you share what you're learning, clearly define leadership as influence for others. They need to understand the context of what you are teaching and understand they *are* leaders (people with influence) too. If you truly want to learn and apply leadership principles, you must start teaching this material to others within 24-48 hours of learning it yourself.

You will learn the foundational principles of leadership (influence) which will help you understand the importance of the following five questions. You will be able to take effective action by growing yourself and possibly others to a higher level of leadership (influence). Everything you ever achieve, internally and externally, will be a direct result of your influence.

1. ***Why*** **do we influence?** – Our character determines *why* we influence. Who we are on the inside is what matters. Do we manipulate or motivate? It's all about our intent.

2. ***How*** **do we influence?** – Our character, combined with our competency, determines *how* we influence. Who we are and what we know combine to create our unique style of influence which determines our methods of influence.

3. ***Where*** **do we influence?** – Our passion and purpose determine *where* we have the greatest influence. What motivates and inspires us gives us the energy and authenticity to motivate and inspire others.

4. ***Who*** **do we influence?** – We influence those *who* buy-in to us. Only those valuing and seeking what we value and seek will volunteer to follow

us. They give us or deny us permission to influence them based on how well we have developed our character and competency.

5. **When do we influence?** – We influence others *when* they want our influence. We choose when others influence us. Everyone else has the same choice. They decide when to accept or reject our influence.

The first three questions are about the choices we make as we lead (influence) ourselves and others. The last two questions deal more with the choices others will make as they decide first, *if* they will follow us, and second, *when* they will follow us. They will base their choices on *who we are* and *what we know*.

Asking these questions is important. Knowing the answers is more important. But, taking action based on the answers is most important. Cumulatively, the answers to these questions determine our leadership style and our level of influence (leadership).

On a scale of 1-10, your influence can be very low level (1) to very high level (10). But make no mistake, you *are* a leader. You *are* always on the scale. There is a positive and negative scale too. The higher on the scale you are the more effective you are. You will be at different levels with different people at different times depending on many different variables.

Someone thinking they are not a leader or someone that doesn't want to be a leader is still a leader. They will simply remain a low impact leader with low level influence getting low level results. They will likely spend much time frustrated with many areas of their life. Although they could influence a change, they choose instead to be primarily influenced by others.

What separates high impact leaders from low impact leaders? There are many things, but two primary differences are:

1) High impact leaders accept more responsibility in all areas of their lives while low impact leaders tend to blame others and transfer responsibility more often.

2) High impact leaders have more positive influence while low impact leaders tend to have more negative influence.

My passion has led me to grow into my purpose which is to help others increase their influence personally and professionally while setting and reaching their goals. I am very passionate and have great conviction. I have realized many benefits by getting better results in all areas of my life. I have improved relationships with my family members, my friends, my associates, my peers, and my clients. I have witnessed people within these same groups embrace leadership principles and reap the same benefits.

The degree to which I *live* what I teach determines my effectiveness. My goal is to learn it, live it, and *then* teach it. I had major internal struggles as I grew my way to where I am. I'm a long way from perfect, so I seek daily improvement. Too often, I see people teaching leadership but not living what they're teaching. If I teach it, I live it.

My goal is to be a better leader tomorrow than I am today. I simply must get out of my own way and lead. I must lead me effectively before I can lead others effectively, not only with acquired knowledge, but also with experience from applying and living the principles.

I'll be transparent with personal stories to help you see how I have applied leadership principles by sharing: How

I've struggled. How I've learned. How I've sacrificed. And, how I've succeeded.

Go beyond highlighting or underlining key points. Take the time to write down your thoughts related to the principle. Write down what you want to change. Write down how you can apply the principle in your life. You may want to consider getting a journal to fully capture your thoughts as you progress through the chapters. What you are thinking as you read is often much more important than what you're reading.

Most importantly, do not focus your thoughts on others. Yes, they need it too. We all need it. I need it. You need it. However, if you focus outside of yourself, you are missing the very point. Your influence comes from within. Your influence rises and falls based on your choices. You have untapped and unlimited potential waiting to be released. Only you can release it.

You, like everyone else, were born a leader. Now, let's take a leadership journey together.

(If you enjoyed this Introduction to *Defining Influence*, it is available in paperback, audio, and as an eBook on Amazon.com or for a signed copy you can purchase at TopStoryLeadership.com.)

Excerpt (Chapter 3 of 30) from
Blue-Collar Leadership® & Culture:
The 5 Components for Building High Performance Teams

THE IMPACT OF CULTURE

THOSE WHO WORK THERE WILL DETERMINE WHO WANTS TO WORK THERE

"I think the most important and difficult thing is to create a culture in the organization where leadership is really important. It's important for people in the company to realize that this is a growth-oriented company, and the biggest thing we have to grow here is you, because it's you who will make this company better by your own growth. ~ Jim Blanchard

Listen to the voices of leaders who are losing the labor war:

- "We just can't find any good people."
    As if…there aren't any good or great people.
- "Due to the low unemployment rate, there just aren't any good people left."
    As if…the only people who can be offered a job are those without a job.
- "In today's labor market, those who want to work are already working."
    As if…those who are working at one place can't decide to work at a different place.

- "When we do get good people, they won't stay."
  As if...the problem is always with the people and never with their leaders.

One thing I know about leaders who make these and similar comments is this: Their culture is a competitive disadvantage. Someone else has the advantage and is winning the battle for the good and great people. The good and great people certainly aren't out of work wishing they had a job. They're working someplace else.

Until a leader is aware of the problem, they can't address the problem. In case it's not obvious, the problem is their culture. The leader owns this problem whether they want to or not. Every time I hear these comments, and I hear them a lot, I know I'm talking to a leader who doesn't know what they don't know.

Ria and I hear leaders across varying blue-collar and white-collar industries repeatedly making these comments as we travel across the USA speaking on leadership development. These voices seem to be getting louder and louder. In fact, these voices are an inspiration for this book.

There are many leaders in blue-collar industries needing help. I want to help them stop searching for good people and start attracting great people. The transformation won't happen overnight. However, until it starts happening, it's not going to happen. My intention is to use this book to raise awareness while providing a transformational road map for those leaders who want to make their culture their greatest competitive advantage.

We were speaking in Louisville, KY recently to owners of blue-collar organizations. Afterward, one approached and said, "There isn't a magic pill is there? I think we all hoped there was." I replied, "No sir. There isn't a magic pill or an easy button. This is how you build a high performance team and an exceptional culture that will attract, retain, and support them. There is no other way."

Your culture is always attracting certain types of people and repelling others. Who we are is who we attract. This principle applies to individuals as well as organizations. The culture within your organization is negatively or positively impacting those within the organization, and some who are outside the organization.

The key point is to understand the people inside your organization are constantly providing the most influential type of advertising about your organization and the leaders within it. It's called word of mouth advertising. How your team is feeling inside the organization will determine what they're saying outside the organization.

If what they're saying about their leaders and the organization to others is good, it'll be easier to find good people. If what they're saying is great, it'll be easier to attract great people. But, if what they're saying is bad, finding good people will be hard, if not impossible.

Remember the voices at the start of this chapter? Those leaders had team members who were sharing bad word of mouth advertising about the organization. Unless those leaders choose to change, nothing will change.

Common sense reveals it's easier to win the labor war while attracting great people instead of searching for good people. However, what's common sense isn't always common practice. Often, it takes uncommon sense to act on things that are commonly understood. Creating an organizational culture that will attract and retain great people requires leaders with uncommon sense.

The best led companies aren't impacted by labor shortages because they're consistently attracting the best and the brightest people to their organizations.

EXCERPT FROM STRAIGHT TALK: THE POWER OF EFFECTIVE COMMUNICATION, BY RIA STORY

I was nearly 20 years old before I realized I liked people. I never considered myself to be an "introvert" although most people would have. I simply didn't talk to people. Ask me a question, and you would get a monosyllabic response that discouraged any further dialogue. It's not that I didn't want to talk or communicate with people – I simply didn't know how.

I grew up very isolated, living on a farm in the middle of the woods. I was homeschooled. We didn't attend church regularly, and my social contact growing up was mainly limited to field trips with other homeschoolers. In the early 1980's in Alabama, opportunities for homeschooled children to participate in extra-curricular activities were limited, and my parents didn't pursue most of them.

I was also sexually abused by my father from age 12 – 19. Growing up with feelings of shame, guilt, hurt, and unworthiness only compounded my natural tendency to be withdrawn, even after I left home at 19. I share more about my story in some of my other books, *Ria's Story From Ashes To Beauty* and *Beyond Bound and Broken: A Journey of Healing and Resilience*.

Leaving home without a job, a car, or even a high school diploma, I got a crash course on the need for communication in "normal" society.

At 19, I had a great education, ability to think critically, reasoning skills, proactive attitude, and willingness to work hard. What I didn't have was the critical ability to connect with other people and communicate *effectively*.

Since I didn't have a GED or a high school diploma,

finding a way to make a living wasn't going to be easy, but I was determined to start making money and earning my way.

My first job was working as a server at a pizza restaurant. I worked the lunch shift, Monday through Friday every day, from 11:00 – 2:00. Most customers would have the all-you-can-eat pizza and salad buffet because it was fast and didn't cost too much.

I was the only lunch server for all 36 tables in the restaurant. My job was to set up the buffet, keep the salad bar stocked and clean, make the tea, fill the ice bin, stock the soda machine, answer the phone, take delivery orders, greet the customers when they entered, take and fill their drink orders, keep dirty plates bussed, refill their drinks, check them out at the cash register, clean the tables, chairs, and floor after the customer left, wash all the dishes, put them away, and restock everything before I left. All for $2.13 per hour, plus any tips I made.

The lunch buffet was $5.99, and a drink was $1.35. Most customer bills came to less than $8.00 for lunch. The average tip is 10% for a buffet, so the best tip I could expect would be about $1.00 – and that's if I hustled really hard to keep their soda refilled and the dirty plates bussed. If I was too busy and the customer ran out of tea, I may not have gotten a tip at all.

I learned quickly that being an "introverted" waitress wasn't going to work. If I didn't smile at the customers, they thought I was unfriendly. If I didn't greet them enthusiastically, they didn't feel welcome or appreciated. If I didn't remember the names of the regular customers and what they liked to drink, they often wouldn't even leave me the change from their dollar.

I learned a lot of things during my years of waiting tables, off and on earlier in my career. You see the best and the worst of people when you wait tables. But, the most important lesson I learned was to take initiative and connect with my customers. **Communicating information wasn't enough. I had to connect with them.** I could tell them where to get a plate and take their drink order, but how I did it made all the difference in whether they left me anything at all, or sometimes, several dollars.

What I want to share with you in this book are some of the lessons I've learned about connecting with people and communicating effectively. There aren't any shortcuts to success, but I hope I can help you avoid the detours and map out a faster route.

Effective communication skills are critical to our success in life.

On the professional side, the ability to communicate and relate to customers, co-workers, employees, or your boss can determine your career potential and define your success.

On the personal side, communication with your spouse, children, parents, and friends will determine your satisfaction in life (at least some of it) and define your relationships.

Regardless of your preferred personality style, or whether you consider yourself an introvert or extrovert, dealing with other people is a fact of life. Almost any situation you can think of requires you to come in contact and interact with other people sooner or later.

Your eye color cannot be changed. Your genetic ability to run a four-minute mile cannot be changed. Your ability to communicate CAN be changed. **Communication is a skill anyone can learn, and everyone can learn to do it better.**

CHAPTER SEVEN OF STRAIGHT TALK:
WINNING THE NAME GAME

"Remember that a person's name is to that person the sweetest and most important sound in any language."

~Dale Carnegie

I meet a lot of people. I meet someone new every day, and sometimes, many people in a single day. I've learned a secret. The greatest way to quickly communicate to someone you care about them is to ask for and remember their name.

I know – some of you will immediately think, "I'm not very good with names."

You won't be good at remembering someone's name until you try. You certainly won't be good at remembering someone's name if you tell yourself you can't, and therefore don't make any effort to do so. Notice you don't have any trouble remembering the names of people you meet who are important, like your new boss, or someone you are excited to meet, maybe a local celebrity.

Remembering names, especially when you meet a lot of people, is a challenge for everyone. Here are some things that help me remember names:

1) **When you meet someone, immediately repeat their name.** If someone at the Chamber Networking event introduces themselves as "Sue," then respond with "It's very nice to meet you *Sue*."
2) **Associate the name to someone else you know.**

It's strange how the brain works, but it will help you remember their name if, as soon as you meet them, you think of someone else you know with that name. The brain will cognitively recognize something that is familiar, and it will make it easier to remember their name the next time you see them. Think to yourself, "Tiffani, like my cousin Tiffani."

3) **Think of something you can associate with them and their name.** For example, if you meet someone named Sally, think of "Sally, like Sally who sold seashells by the seashore." It seems silly, but it will connect the dots allowing you to remember her name by saying it in a way that causes it to stick.

4) **Ask how they spell it.** There is almost always more than one way to spell a name. When you hear it spelled out, stop and visualize how it looks in your mind. This really helps, especially if it's a name that is not common. I often repeat it back to them. For example, when I meet someone named "Cathy," I ask if it's spelled with a "C" or a "K." She may reply, "Cathy with a C," and I repeat it back, "Nice to meet you Cathy with a C!" Note – if the person's name is very simple, like "Dan," this is probably not a great tool to use.

5) **Write it down.** It's not always possible, but in some settings this can be very helpful. For example, if I'm getting ready to teach a class and I meet someone new, I might jot their name down on my notes for quick reference when I teach the class again next week. By then, an entire week will have passed, and I will remember the person's face, but I may not remember their name. But, I will remember I wrote it down and can quickly remind myself to check if needed.

6) **Ask them to tell you something unique about themselves.** It's a great icebreaker question anyway. "It's great to meet you Melissa. Tell me something unique about yourself." If the person isn't sure how to

answer, you can follow up with "Tell me something you are passionate about." Or ask, "What's the craziest thing you've ever done?"

7) **Associate them with someone famous.** Obviously not everyone will have a name similar to someone famous. But, when it happens, it makes it easy to remember. "It's nice to meet you Teresa. Were you named after the famous Mother Teresa?"

8) **Ask how they got their name.** Maybe they don't have a name like someone famous, but asking where their name originated is a good way to connect with them. "It's a pleasure to meet you Miranda. What caused your parents to choose that name for you? Is it a family name?"

Make every effort to remember a person's name when you meet them. If you don't remember, it's best to acknowledge it, apologize, and ask again. But, if you do this, you absolutely MUST remember it from then on. Don't make them tell you a third time.

One more thing about names – get into the habit of introducing yourself to someone so that your name is easy to remember. Say it so it sticks.

I think the best example I know of is how my husband Mack introduces himself. He says, "My name is Mack, like the truck, but smaller." It never fails – people remember his name because he gives them a visual image and an emotional connection to tie it to. It may take you a little time to come up with something "sticky" about your name, but it's well worth it. My name is Ria, like Kia the car but with an "R."

READ MORE BOOKS BY MACK AND RIA

The Effective Leadership Series books are written to develop and enhance your leadership skills, while also helping you increase your abilities in areas like communication and relationships, time management, planning and execution, leading and implementing change. Look for more books in the Effective Leadership Series:

- Straight Talk: The Power of Effective Communication
- Change Happens: Leading Yourself and Others through Change
- PRIME Time: The Power of Effective Planning
- Leadership Gems: 30 Characteristics of Very Successful Leaders
- Leadership Gems for Women: 30 Characteristics of Very Successful Women

It's easier to compete when you're attracting great people instead of searching for good people.

Blue-Collar Leadership® & Culture will help you understand why culture is the key to becoming a sought after employer of choice within your industry and in your area of operation.

You'll also discover how to leverage the components of The Transformation Equation to create a culture that will support, attract, and retain high performance team members.

Blue-Collar Leadership® & Culture is intended to serve as a tool, a guide, and a transformational road map for leaders who want to create a high impact culture that will become their greatest competitive advantage.

READ MORE BOOKS BY MACK AND RIA

Note: Leadership Gems is the generic, non-gender specific, version of Leadership Gems for Women. The content is very similar.

One of the greatest leadership myths is that you must be a "born" leader to be successful. In truth, leadership and influence are skills that can be developed and improved. However, to be very successful, you must intentionally develop your skills so you can lead and influence others at work, in your career, at home, church, or even as a volunteer.

In Leadership Gems, Ria has packed 30 precious gems of leadership wisdom on characteristics of very successful leaders - and insight on how you can develop them yourself. These lessons will help you become a very successful leader regardless of whether you are in a formal leadership position or not.

READ MORE BOOKS BY MACK AND RIA

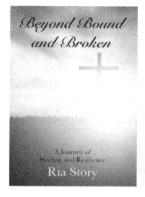

Ria Story

In Beyond Bound and Broken, Ria shares how she overcame shame, fear, and doubt that stemmed from years of being sexually abused by her father. Forced to play the role of a wife and even shared with other men due to her father's perversions, Ria left home at 19 without a job, a car, or even a high-school diploma. This book also contains lessons on resilience and overcoming adversity that you can apply to your own life.

In Ria's Story From Ashes To Beauty, Ria tells her story of growing as a victim of sexual abuse from age 12 – 19, and leaving home to escape. She shares how she went on to thrive and learn to help others by sharing her story.

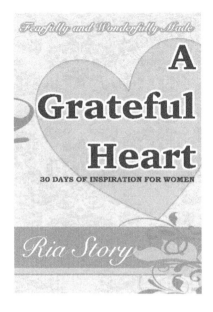

Become inspired by this 30-day collection of daily devotions for women, where you will find practical advice on intentionally living with a grateful heart, inspirational quotes, short journaling opportunities, and scripture from God's Word on practicing gratitude.

READ MORE BOOKS BY MACK AND RIA

"I wish someone had given me these books 30 years ago when I started my career on the front lines. They would have changed my life then. They can change your life now." ~ Mack Story

Blue-Collar Leadership® & Supervision and *Blue-Collar Leadership®* are written specifically for those who lead the people on the frontlines and for those on the front lines. With 30 short, easy to read 3 page chapters, these books contain powerful, yet simple to understand leadership lessons.

Down load the first 5 chapters of each book FREE at: BlueCollarLeadership.com

READ MORE BOOKS BY MACK AND RIA

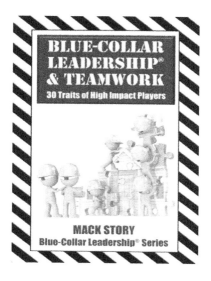

Are you ready to play at the next level and beyond?

In today's high stakes game of business, the players on the team are the competitive advantage for any organization. But, only if they are on the field instead of on the bench.

The competitive advantage for every individual is developing 360° of influence regardless of position, title, or rank.

Blue-Collar Leadership® & *Teamwork* provides a simple, yet powerful and unique, resource for individuals who want to increase their influence and make a high impact. It's also a resource and tool for leaders, teams, and organizations, who are ready to Engage the Front Line to Improve the Bottom Line.

READ MORE BOOKS BY MACK AND RIA

The biggest challenge in process improvement and cultural transformation isn't identifying the problems. It's execution: implementing and sustaining the solutions.

Blue-Collar Kaizen is a resource for anyone in any position who is, or will be, leading a team through process improvement and change. Learn to engage, empower, and encourage your team for long term buy-in and sustained gains.

Mack Story has over 11,000 hours experience leading hundreds of leaders and thousands of their cross-functional kaizen team members through process improvement, organizational change, and cultural transformation.

Mack's MAXIMIXE Your Potential and MAXIMIZE Your Leadership Potential books are the white-collar version of the Blue-Collar Leadership® Series. MAXIMIZE Your Potential books are written specifically for those working on the front lines and those who lead them. With 30 short, easy to read chapters, they contain powerful leadership lessons in a simple and easy to understand format.

Everything rises and falls on influence. Nothing will impact your professional and personal life more than your ability to influence others. Are you looking for better results in your life, team, or organization? In Defining Influence, everyone at all levels will learn the keys to increase their influence.

It's no longer "Buyer Beware!" It's "Seller Beware!" Why? Today, the buyer has the advantage over the seller. Most often they are holding it in their hand. It's a smart phone. They can learn everything about your product before they meet you. The major advantage you do still have is: YOU!

This book is filled with 30 short chapters providing unique insights that will give you the advantage, not over the buyer, but over your competition: those who are selling what you're selling. It will help you sell yourself.

READ MORE BOOKS BY MACK AND RIA

High impact leaders align their habits with key values in order to maximize their influence. High impact leaders intentionally grow and develop themselves in an effort to more effectively grow and develop others. These *10 Values* are commonly understood. However, they are not always commonly practiced. These *10 Values* will help you build trust and accelerate relationship building. Those mastering these *10 Values* will be able to lead with speed as they develop 360° of influence from wherever they are.

READ MORE BOOKS BY MACK AND RIA

10 Foundational Elements of Intentional Transformation serves as a source of motivation and inspiration to help you climb your way to the next level and beyond as you learn to intentionally create a better future for yourself. The pages will ENCOURAGE, ENGAGE, and EMPOWER you as you become more focused and intentional about moving from where you are to where you want to be.

All of us are somewhere, but most of us want to be somewhere else. However, we don't always know how to get there. You will learn how to intentionally move forward as you learn to navigate the 10 foundational layers of transformation.

READ MORE BOOKS BY MACK AND RIA

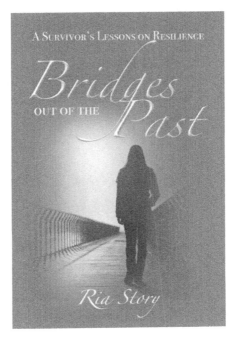

It's not what happens to you in life. It's who you become because of it. We all experience pain, grief, and loss in life. Resilience is the difference between *"I didn't die,"* and *"I learned to live again."* In this captivating book on resilience, Ria walks you through her own horrific story of more than seven years of sexual abuse by her father. She then shares how she learned not only to survive, but also to thrive in spite of her past. Learn how to overcome challenges, obstacles, and adversity in your own life by building a bridge out of the past and into the future.

READ MORE BOOKS BY MACK AND RIA

You have hopes, dreams, and goals you want to achieve. You have aspirations of leaving a legacy of significance. You have untapped potential waiting to be unleashed.

But, unfortunately, how to maximize your potential isn't something addressed in job or skills training. And sadly, how to achieve success and find significance in life isn't something taught in school, college, or by most parents.

In *ACHIEVE: Maximize Your Potential with 7 Keys to Unlock Success and Significance,* Ria shares lessons on Attitude, Choices, Humility, Integrity, Energy, Vision, and Excellence. Each "key" can help you become more influential, more successful and maximize your potential in life.

ABOUT MACK STORY

Mack's story is an amazing journey of personal and professional growth. He married Ria in 2001. He has one son, Eric, born in 1991.

After graduating high school in 1987, Mack joined the United States Marine Corps Reserve as an 0311 infantryman. Soon after, he began his 20 plus year manufacturing career. Graduating with highest honors, he earned an Executive Bachelor of Business Administration degree from Faulkner University.

Mack began his career in manufacturing in 1988 on the front lines of a large production machine shop. He eventually grew himself into upper management and found his niche in lean manufacturing and along with it, developed his passion for leadership. In 2008, he launched his own Lean Manufacturing and Leadership Development firm.

From 2005-2012, Mack led leaders and their cross-functional teams through more than 11,000 hours of process improvement, organizational change, and cultural transformation.

In 2013, Mack and his wife Ria worked with John C. Maxwell as part of an international training event focused on the Cultural Transformation in Guatemala where over 20,000 leaders were trained. They also shared the stage with internationally recognized motivational speaker Les Brown in 2014.

Mack and Ria have published 20+ books on personal growth and leadership development. In 2018, they were invited to speak at Yale University's School of Management. Mack and Ria inspire people everywhere through their example of achievement, growth, and personal development.

Clients: ATD (Association for Talent Development), Auburn University, Chevron, Chick-fil-A, Kimberly Clark, Koch Industries, Southern Company, and the U.S. Military.

ABOUT RIA STORY

Like many, Ria faced adversity in life. Ria was sexually abused by her father from age 12 - 19, forced to play the role of his wife, and even trafficked to other men. Desperate to escape, she left home at 19 without a job, a car, or even a high school diploma. Ria learned to be resilient, not only surviving, but thriving. She worked her way through college, earning her MBA with a cumulative 4.0 GPA, and had a successful career in the corporate world of administrative healthcare.

Today, Ria is a motivational leadership speaker, TEDx Speaker, and author of 11 books, including Leadership Gems for Women. Ria was selected three times to speak on stage at International John Maxwell Certification Events. Motivational speaker Les Brown also invited Ria to share the stage with him in Los Angeles, CA. Ria is a member of the Georgia Statewide Human Trafficking Task Force.

Ria is a certified leadership speaker and trainer with nearly 20 years of experience in leadership and management. Clients include: ATD (Association for Talent Development), Auburn University, Chevron, Chick-fil-A, Kimberly Clark, and the U.S. Military.

Ria founded Fearfully and Wonderfully Me. Ria shares powerful leadership principles and tools of transformation from her journey to equip and empower women, helping them maximize their potential in life and leadership.

WHAT WE OFFER:

- ✓ Keynote Speaking: Conferences, Seminars, Onsite
- ✓ Workshops: Onsite/Offsite Half/Full/Multi Day
- ✓ Leadership Development Support: Leadership, Teamwork, Personal Growth, Organizational Change, Planning, Executing, Trust, Cultural Transformation, Communication, Time Management, Selling with Character, Resilience, & Relationship Building
- ✓ Blue-Collar Leadership® Development
- ✓ Corporate Retreats
- ✓ Women's Retreat (with Ria Story)
- ✓ Limited one-on-one coaching/mentoring
- ✓ On-site Lean Leadership Certification
- ✓ Lean Leader Leadership Development
- ✓ Become licensed to teach our content

FOR MORE INFORMATION PLEASE VISIT:

BlueCollarLeadership.com
TopStoryLeadership.com

FOLLOW US ON SOCIAL MEDIA:

LinkedIn.com/in/MackStory
Facebook.com/Mack.Story

LinkedIn.com/in/RiaStory
Facebook.com/Ria.Story

LISTEN/SUBSCRIBE TO OUR PODCASTS AT:
TopStoryLeadership.com/Podcast

ENGAGE Your
FRONT LINE
To IMPROVE the
BOTTOM LINE!

If you're willing to invest in your
Blue-Collar team, I am too!

~Mack Story

Limited Time Special Offer:

Take advantage of our "Special Offer
Package" with a reduced speaking fee of
ONLY $3,600, and receive 200 books from
our Blue-Collar Leadership® Series FREE!
For details, visit:
BlueCollarLeadership.com/Special-Offer

*Restrictions apply.

*"My first words are, GET SIGNED UP! This
training is not, and I stress, not your everyday
leadership seminar!" Sam, VP & COO*